Research and survey in
nature conservation series
Report No 11
A woodland survey handbook

No. 11

A woodland survey handbook

K J Kirby

Further copies of this report can be obtained from
Publicity Services Branch, Nature Conservancy Council,
Northminster House, Peterborough PE1 1UA

Research and survey in nature conservation series

No. 1   The use of permanent quadrats to record changes in the structure and composition of Wytham Woods, Oxfordshire. A S Horsfall and K J Kirby. 1985. £1.00.

No. 2   Monitoring the abundance of butterflies 1976-1985. E Pollard, M L Hall and T J Bibby. 1986. £6.50.

No. 3   Saltmarsh survey of Great Britain: Bibliography.   Compiled by Kevin Charman, Wanda Fojt and Shirley Penny. 1986. £2.00.

No. 4   A survey of the numbers and breeding distribution of the North Atlantic gannet Sula bassana and an assessment of the changes which have occurred since Operation Seafarer 1969/70. Sarah Wanless. 1987. £3.00.

No. 5   Agricultural structures policy and nature conservation in Upland Grampian: a pilot study. J R Crabtree, Sue Evans, Brian J Revell and Philip M K Leat. 1987. £2.00.

No. 6   Changes in the Cumbrian countryside. First report of the National Countryside Monitoring Scheme. 1987. £3.50.

No. 7   The Wash and its environment. Report of a conference held on 8-10 April 1987 at Horncastle, Lincolnshire. Edited by Pat Doody and Brian Barnett. 1987. £5.00.

No. 8   The moths of Ceredigion. A P Fowles. 1988. £5.00.

No. 9   Long-term monitoring in unmanaged woodland nature reserves. G F Peterken and Christa Backmeroff. 1988. £2.50.

No. 10   The woods of Argyll and Bute. Jane MacKintosh. 1988. £3.50.

No. 11   A woodland survey handbook. K J Kirby. 1988. £6.50.

No. 12   The reintroduction of the white-tailed sea eagle to Scotland: 1975-1987. Prepared by John A Love. 1988. £4.00.

No. 13   Saltmarsh vegetation of the Wash. An assessment of change from 1971 to 1985. Margaret I Hill. 1988. £4.50.

No. 14   The peatland management handbook. T A Rowell. 1988. £6.00.

Summary

This book provides an introduction to woodland survey for nature conservation. It summarises much of the experience gained from surveys carried out by the Nature Conservancy Council and Nature Conservation Trusts over the last ten years. The main emphasis is on field surveys using vascular plant records to give a preliminary assessment of a wood's nature conservation value. Other types of survey from broadscale desk studies to detailed examination of epiphytic lichen communities are also discussed.

Acknowledgements

I wish to thank the many colleagues within the NCC who contributed their ideas to this book, in particular Tony Mitchell-Jones (mammals), Ian McLean, Alan Stubbs and Peter Wormell (invertebrates), Ray Woods (epiphytes), Colin Ranson (soil surface features) and Lynne Farrell (rare plant monitoring). I am also grateful to Dr J Rodwell (Lancaster University) and Dr R J Fuller (British Trust for Ornithology), who provided the sections on the National Vegetation Classification and bird surveys respectively. Dr R G H Bunce and J M Sykes of the Institute of Terrestrial Ecology provided me with copious data and good advice. Numerous other authors and journal editors have kindly allowed us to reproduce figures and tables. Finally, I thank Lissie Wright and Philip Oswald for editing the text for publication.

Contents

	Page
Introduction	9
Aims and levels of woodland survey	10
Objectives of woodland nature conservation in Britain	10
Objectives of woodland surveys for nature conservation	10
The woodland resource	10
Levels of woodland survey	11
Standardisation of survey results	13
Survey accuracy	13
Unplanned surveys	13
Conclusions	14
Broadscale (Level 1) surveys	15
Introduction	15
Inventories of ancient semi-natural woodland	15
Habitat mapping	17
Canopy cover surveys	18
Forestry Commission censuses	22
Other surveys	23
Use of Level 1 surveys	23
Conclusions	23
Site (Level 2) surveys – general points	26
Introduction	26
What do you record?	27
Vascular plant recording in woodlands	29
Plant parameters	29
Sampling methods	29
Species listing on walks	29
Use of the DAFOR scale for species abundance assessment	33
Species listing from quadrats – number and size of quadrat	34
Random, systematic, stratified random and subjective plot positions	34
Estimates of species abundance based on quadrats	40
Walks or quadrats – which method?	42
Other factors affecting species recording	42
Indicator species	45
Mapping and classifying vegetation	46
Introduction	46
Classification and mapping	48
Classification systems	52
Which classification to use?	53
Relationships between types from the different systems	53
Whole site classifications	56
Sub-site recording	57
Woodland structure	59
Introduction	59
Natural structures	59
Structure, diversity and management	59
Assessment of structure	59
Conclusions	60
Subsidiary habitats within woodland	65

Species groups other than vascular plants (general)   68
     Introduction   68
     The use of lower plants in woodland classification   69

Mammals   70
     Introduction   70
     Small mammals   70
     Medium-sized insectivores, rodents and lagomorphs   72
     Carnivores   73
     Deer   74
     Grazing surveys   74

Invertebrates   75
     Introduction   75
     General points   75
     Woodland site factors   76
     Scrub relics and isolated trees   78

Birds   79
     Introduction   79
     Habitat features   79
     Methods of counting birds   80
     Territory mapping   81

Epiphytes, particularly lichens   83
     Introduction   83
     Initial surveys   83
     Recording communities   85
     Site evaluation   86

Management   88

Soils   90
     Texture   90
     Structure   92
     Drainage   92
     pH   93
     Organic horizons   93
     Soil mineral layers   94
     Soil classification   95
     Guidelines for soil recording for woodland surveyors   96

Soil surface features   97

Monitoring   101
     Introduction   101
     Plots and transects   102
     Photographic monitoring   103
     Rare plant monitoring   104
     Other types of monitoring   105
     Conclusions   105

Publication and publicity   106

Appendices   107
    1   Woodland evaluation   109
    2   General hints on survey organisation   111
    3   Recording forms and instructions   113
    4   Main classification systems   133

References   151

List of tables

Table 1   Output from the Ancient Woodland Inventory Project   15
Table 2   Results from a canopy survey of Scottish deciduous woodland   18
Table 3   Part of the county results from the Forestry Commission's
           1979-82 census   22
Table 4   Some sources of information on woodlands at a county level   24
Table 5   Criteria for judging nature conservation value and their
           relationship to commonly recorded woodland features   28
Table 6   Number of species detected on six walks through a wood when
           the length of route remained the same in each case but the
           actual path followed varied each time   32
Table 7   Comparison of subjective cover estimates with frequency
           data from quadrat surveys   33
Table 8   The relationship between quadrat size, quadrat number and
           the number of plant species detected   35
Table 9   The sampling percentages achieved by varying numbers of 200 m²
           quadrats in woods of different sizes   35
Table 10   Variability in the total number of species recorded from small
           sets of quadrats   37
Table 11   A comparison of different silvicultural treatments in Salcey
           Forest, based on 10 randomly placed quadrats in each treatment   37
Table 12   A comparison of unrestricted random and stratified random
           sampling for the detection of plot types and plant species   40
Table 13   The effect of observer efficiency and season indicated by
           species in common between pairs of lists   43
Table 14   Species or genera which may be missed or misidentified in surveys 44
Table 15   Similarity of the ground flora (1974–1984) from 21 plots in
           Wytham Woods (Oxon)   45
Table 16   Classification of woodlands used in A nature conservation review 52
Table 17   Examples of the relationships between different classification systems 54
Table 18   Sub-site records   57
Table 19   Woodland structure   61
Table 20   Part of a recording form for subsidiary habitats within woodland 65
Table 21   Subsidiary habitats within woodland   67
Table 22   Basic bryophyte and lichen list   69
Table 23   British mammals and their preferred woodland habitats   71
Table 24   Information included on an epiphytic community recording sheet   85
Table 25   Indications of management, past and present   89
Table 26   Texture assessment in soils   91
Table 27   Regeneration survey in eight-year-old enclosures in Great Wood,
           Borrowdale (Cumbria)   103
Table 28   A framework for woodland evaluation   110

List of figures Page

Figure 1   Comparison between different levels of survey   12
Figure 2   Ways of dividing up British woodland   16
Figure 3   Habitat map   17
Figure 4   Results from a canopy survey of Scottish deciduous woodland   19
Figure 5   Forestry Commission surveys and censuses   20
Figure 6   Woodland distribution patterns at a county level   25
Figure 7   Output from a Level 2 survey   26
Figure 8   Various "plant parameters" for a wood   30
Figure 9   The relationship between the time spent recording and the number
            of species found on a walk and in quadrat surveys   31
Figure 10   Possible survey routes in woodland   32
Figure 11   The relationship between the number of species found and the size
            and the number of quadrats recorded   36
Figure 12   Species distribution and cover based on a systematic sampling pattern   38
Figure 13   Use of Domin values to compare species abundance in different
            parts of a wood   41
Figure 14   Distribution maps   46
Figure 15   Different ways of approaching the classification problem   47
Figure 16   Mapping of individual features and small-scale variation within
            an area of comparatively uniform woodland   48
Figure 17   A hypothetical comparison of the results from free and sample
            point mapping   49
Figure 18   The effect of scale of sampling on distribution maps   50
Figure 19   Distribution of a "rare event" in a woodland, mapped by complete survey   51
Figure 20   Possible limitations to "Site Type" classifications   56
Figure 21   Stages in sub-site recording   58
Figure 22   Recording woodland structure in Level 2 surveys   62
Figure 23   Examples of results from detailed structural surveys   63
Figure 24   Tree diameter distributions   64
Figure 25   Characterisation of rides as habitats for invertebrates   66
Figure 26   The relationship between the number of vascular plants recorded
            from a wood and bryophyte cover   68
Figure 27   Example of bird territory mapping results   82
Figure 28   Earthworks in a wood   98
Figure 29   Monitoring changes after felling, using permanent plots   101
Figure 30   Diagram of a "real" quadrat   126

Introduction

This handbook examines woodland survey for nature conservation, concentrating on the methods used to provide a broad assessment of the wildlife interest of a wood. It is a development of CST Note 2, Woodland survey for nature conservation (Peterken 1977a), and the survey chapters in Peterken (1981). It is written primarily for NCC staff, but I hope it will interest and be useful to people outside the organisation. It complements the volume on grassland survey methods by Smith, Wells & Welsh (1985) and is mainly relevant to British conditions. Those interested in wider aspects might consult Myers, Margules & Musto (1983) or Clarke (1986).

Nature conservation surveys in woodlands may cover a wide range of features from the soil to the forest structure. My aim has been to illustrate possible survey methods or approaches and give appropriate references for those who wish to know more about any particular one. The first section of the book deals with the background to nature conservation surveys in woodland and the second with broadscale surveys. Later sections cover a series of topics in turn in more detail - for example plant recording, vegetation classification and mapping, and woodland structure. Numerous tables and figures have been included because it is easier to judge whether a particular method is what you want if you can see examples of the results. In general I have excluded experimental studies and statistical analysis; those who wish to pursue these subjects might start by consulting Jeffers (1978a, b).

The results from ecological and forestry research on sampling methods have been helpful in devising nature conservation survey methods, but the practicalities of collecting information from many sites in varying ownerships with limited resources have also to be considered. No apology is made therefore for the apparent crudity of some of the methods.

A joint NCC/ITE study group (Anon. 1974) identified six stages in a survey - definition of objectives, design of project, collection of data, interpretation of data, storage of data, and application of results. This book is mainly concerned with the second, third and fourth stages. Definition of objectives is crucial, but it should be done before turning to a book of methods. The use of survey results to assess the value of a wood for nature conservation is discussed briefly in Appendix 1 but is dealt with in detail elsewhere, for example by Goodfellow & Peterken (1981), Kirby (1980, 1986), Peterken (1981), Ratcliffe (1977) and Usher (1986).

Hints on organising surveys are contained in Appendix 2. Examples of the general woodland recording forms that have been used within the Nature Conservancy Council for the last few years and the relevant instructions for completing them are given in Appendix 3. (Minor modifications, for example to take account of species name changes, are in progress.)

This book is not intended to be the "final word" on nature conservation surveys. The next few years will see the adoption of the National Vegetation Classification within the NCC as a means of characterising woods. Simple techniques for monitoring long-term changes in woods need further investigation. Computer storage of the results from woodland conservation surveys is slowly becoming more common and this will have implications for how data are collected. Any comments or suggestions for improving survey methods and practice will be stored up for a second edition!

Aims and levels of woodland survey

Objectives of woodland nature conservation in Britain

The object of woodland nature conservation in Britain is to maintain as much as possible of what remains of the natural woodland pattern. This pattern consists of the woodland species and communities, their distribution and interactions, as well as the physical features of the woodland, its structure, soils, and the open areas, streams or cliffs found within woods. All woods in Britain have been modified by man to a greater or lesser extent. Nature conservation surveys are concerned with identifying those woods which contain more of the natural woodland pattern than others.

Objectives of woodland surveys for nature conservation

(a)   To define the boundary and extent of those woods which are of particular interest to the Nature Conservancy Council (or to other nature conservation bodies).

(b)   To determine the relative importance for nature conservation of each wood.

(c)   To assist with decisions and recommendations for the management of the woods to maintain the more natural elements of the woodland pattern.

(d)   To monitor future changes in the woodland pattern, to determine the rate and direction of past change and thereby to anticipate trends.

(e)   To be able to demonstrate sufficient knowledge about all the woods in a region to justify our description and evaluation of and proposals for a particular wood.

(f)   Less commonly, to identify sites suitable for research and educational uses related to nature conservation.

The woodland resource

There are about two million hectares of woodland and plantations in Britain, all of which contain some wildlife. Much of this occurs as large coniferous plantations and small woods or clumps of trees of less than 2 ha. As a rule neither of these categories contains sites which are individually of great importance for woodland conservation. This leaves woodland sites mostly in the range 2-200 ha, usually more or less isolated from other woodland by stretches of arable ground, pasture, moorland, urban areas etc. The main aim of the NCC's woodland conservation strategy is to try to separate these into broad categories representing different levels of nature conservation importance and to press for appropriate types of forestry treatment for each category so as to maintain that level of wildlife interest (Steele & Peterken 1982). To some extent this has been achieved through the Broadleaves Policy (Forestry Commission 1985a, b). Within the most important categories we need to know which woods should be notified as Sites of Special Scientific Interest or become nature reserves. Within individual woods there may be compartments with important features or species which must receive very precise treatment if these features are not to be destroyed. Thus the nature conservation interest must be defined, through survey, at a variety of scales.

Most British woods have been actively managed in the past. Some types of treatment (both past and present) help to maintain a wide range of native plants and animals as well as other elements of the natural woodland pattern. On the other hand, clearance of woodland and the replanting of semi-natural stands with conifers reduce the nature conservation value of a site. Broadscale surveys indicate how the extent, composition and structure of woods have changed in the recent past. Surveys within woods help to identify particular forestry treatments and systems that are generally beneficial for wildlife. Hence conclusions can be drawn about the effects of past woodland changes, recommendations can be made about present practices, and the implications for nature conservation of future trends can be identified.

Woodlands and their wildlife are a resource which is part of our heritage. To appreciate them we must know where they are, what they contain, and how they originated. Whatever other function they serve, nature conservation surveys should contribute to a better understanding and use of the countryside. This emphasises the need to produce and publish, or at least publicise, survey reports.

Levels of woodland survey

Broad levels of survey can be defined which are distinguished by the amount of information which is collected per site. (See also the discussion in Smith, Wells & Welsh 1985.) This determines the methods employed and the number of sites which can be considered in a given time. There are not the resources to survey all woods to a very high level of detail.

The results from a given level may be used to select the woods to be surveyed at a higher (more detailed) level. Equally, results from detailed surveys of a few sites may be extrapolated to others identified as similar in the lower level surveys (Figure 1). The concept is useful because it helps to define the minimum amount of information that must be collected to meet a particular objective. In practice, levels of survey are not clear-cut, but tend to merge.

Level 1 surveys (often called Phase 1 surveys) are concerned with the total woodland resource and with defining the location and extent of those woods which are of particular nature conservation value (objective (a) above). They provide a basis for monitoring changes in the number and total area of these sites (objective (d)). To a lesser extent they contribute to other objectives.

Level 2 surveys are aimed at defining more precisely the nature conservation interest of particular sites so that a preliminary assessment of their value at local, county or national level can be made (objectives (b) and (e)). This leads to a consideration in broad terms of what is the most appropriate treatment for the site (objective (c)). Studies of the invertebrates, breeding birds or soils usually form part of Level 3 survey programmes because of the time per site that is required. They contribute to objectives (b), (c) and (e). Within-site monitoring is also usually classed as Level 3.

In practical terms, less than an hour might be spent dealing with a site in Level 1 surveys. In Level 2 surveys up to one or two days might be spent in an area of 30-50 hectares. Level 3 surveys may involve weeks, months or years of work, for example the descriptions of the New Forest (Tubbs 1964, 1986), Monks Wood (Steele & Welch 1973), Bedford Purlieus (Peterken & Welch 1975), Hayley Wood (Rackham 1975) and Brasenose Wood (Steel 1984) or of particular types of tree or woodland, such as pinewoods (Steven & Carlisle 1959; Bunce & Jeffers 1977), oak (Morris & Perring 1974), birch (Henderson & Mann 1984) and upland plantations (Hill 1979a; Moss 1979).

Figure 1   Comparison between different levels of survey

Level   Examples of output

Level 1   Often a desk exercise;   Size distribution of woods (shaded
           large number of sites   section indicating surviving
           surveyed; short time per   semi-natural area)
           site; provides general
           information on the size
           and condition of the
           woodland resource

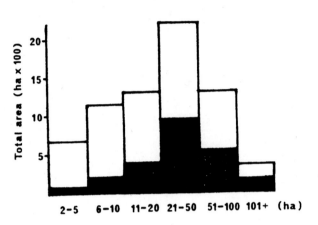

                   Extrapolation to
                   similar sites

                                             Size distribution of ancient woods in Surrey

           Selection of
           sites for
           further survey

Level 2   Field survey giving   Vegetation map and plant list
           preliminary description and
           evaluation of site; classification
           of communities present; initial
           conclusions on desirable
           management

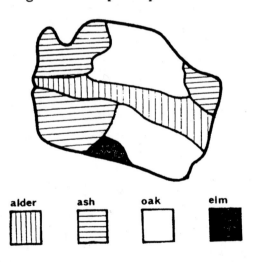

                   Extrapolation to
                   similar sites

           Selection of
           sites for
           further survey

Map of stand types

Level 3   Detailed survey of different   Breeding bird census
           aspects of the wood to define
           its interest fully and   Soil map
           describe the woodland processes
           involved   Enumeration of the trees

                                            Detailed map of plant distributions

Standardisation of survey results

One aim of most surveys is to compare different woods or different silvicultural treatments and draw conclusions about their relative nature conservation value. This can only be done if the results are in some "standard" form and have been obtained in broadly similar ways. Therefore attempts have been made to define standard methods.

If any method is to be applied over a wide area of the country, it must cope with the differences in the nature of the woods between, for example, Suffolk and Argyll. Completely standardised procedures can be devised (e.g. Bunce & Shaw 1973), but they have a cost. Either very little information can be collected per site (since what is collected must all be relevant to all sites) or else much of what is collected is irrelevant for most sites, so that surveys take longer than necessary. In Argyll the bryophyte component of oak woods is often far more important in identifying important sites than the vascular plant list; in Suffolk ash-hazel woods the reverse is true. Insisting on detailed bryophyte records for surveys throughout the country would greatly increase the time required to survey each wood without in many cases substantially improving our judgement of the value of sites. It is better to define a minimum survey framework that applies generally and can be added to according to circumstances or objectives.

Survey accuracy

The limits to the precision of any particular survey method must be appreciated. Methods should give "reliable" and "valid" results (Farr 1974). "Reliability" is a measure of the variability between results obtained from repeated application of the same method to a given site, e.g. the differences in the number of species found on repeated walks through the same wood. "Validity" refers to whether (in this instance) the number of species found on a walk in different woods is always the same proportion of the total species complement for each wood, i.e. to the consistency with which the method detects real differences between woods. A "standard" method does not necessarily have the same level of accuracy in all circumstances.

Potential sources of error should be considered in judging survey methods and their results, for example the competence of the surveyor and variations between surveyors; inconsistencies or differences in interpretation of survey instructions; differences in the sources (for example aerial photographs may be available in some areas but not others); and, in field surveys, weather, season of the year and nature of the terrain. The smallest difference in results between sites that can be judged significant is determined by the size of the errors in the survey methods.

Unplanned surveys

Despite the value of properly designed surveys, it is important to be able to use the results from "unplanned" woodland visits as well. Inevitably casework problems arise in the winter before a site is due to be properly surveyed (Sod's Law, 7th day after Creation). Any woodland visit should therefore be viewed as potentially contributing to one or other of the levels of survey outlined earlier and the necessary minimum amount of information to meet the requirements of that level should be collected. Anything else is a bonus. If the information available from planned or opportunistic surveys does not reach the minimum requirement, some comparisons may still be possible. However, the reliability of the conclusions which may be drawn is correspondingly reduced.

The next section examines Level 1 surveys briefly. Later sections deal with the various components of more detailed surveys.

Conclusions

(a) Objectives must be clearly stated because these determine the type of survey procedure to be adopted.

(b) The concept of different levels of survey is helpful in channelling survey effort into those sites where it will be most useful.

(c) Standard survey methods should be adopted, but some flexibility must be retained to allow for inherent variability within the woods and the need to make use of opportunistic survey information. Results should be presented in a standard way.

(d) Sources of error and variation in the results must be allowed for when assessing differences between sites.

Broadscale (Level 1) surveys

Introduction

An Ordance Survey map provides an immediate way of identifying where the woods are and how big they are. However, it is seldom possible to visit all the sites shown on such maps, nor are they all likely to be of equal interest for nature conservation, so some subdivision is required.

British woodland has been divided up in various ways in an attempt to separate out the sites most likely to be of high value for nature conservation (Figure 2) - into broadleaf versus coniferous (since in most of the country the native woodland is broadleaf); ancient versus recent; semi-natural stands versus plantations; and stands of native trees versus introductions. Level 1 surveys aim to locate all woodland sites somewhere on at least one of these axes of variation. The decision as to which axis to use as the primary division in the survey depends in part on the nature of the woods, in part on the resources available. The extent of secondary division may also vary. It may be more important to distinguish semi-natural stands from plantations on ancient sites than it is on recent sites.

Inventories of ancient semi-natural woodland

Peterken (1977b, 1983) has made the case for treating ancient semi-natural woods as the most important category of woods for nature conservation, and the NCC's surveys to identify and list such woods on a county-by-county basis are described in Kirby et al. (1984) and Walker & Kirby (1987). Examples of the output from this project are given in Table 1. Provisional reports for the whole of Great Britain should be available by the end of 1988.

Table 1   Output from the Ancient Woodland Inventory Project
Information collected on the individual sites as simplified for computer storage

The sites are listed in strict numerical order of grid reference within each 100 km square. The 100 km squares are arranged in alphabetical order on the inventory. Each entry has either one or two lines. The first gives the following:
Name
Parish
Ten kilometre square
Grid reference

Column A	-	The area of "ancient woodland" shown on the 1:25,000 base maps
Column B	-	The area of "ancient woodland" belived to be still extant at the of the inventory
Column C	-	The area of "ancient woodland" thought still to be semi-natural
Column D	-	The area of "ancient woodland" thought to have been replanted
Column E	-	The area cleared since the base maps were drawn
Constat	-	The conservation status of the site

The second line of an entry gives:

| Remarks | - | Other general information |
| Owner | - | When known and only in broad categories |

Name	Parish		A B C D E	Constat
Hales Copse	Frensham	SU83 845394	3 3 3 0 0	
'Silverbeck Wood'	Frensham	SU83 860390	7 6 6 0 1	
'Woodcock Bottom Woods'	Hindhead & Churt	SU83 870359	5 5 5 0 0	
			Owner: NT(part)	

Figure 2   Ways of dividing up British woodland

Sketch map based on the Witherslack area (Cumbria) illustrating different types of woodland

1   Ancient semi-natural broadleaf stands - ash-hazel coppice with oak standards
2   Ancient semi-natural conifer (yew) stands on crags and scree
3   Broadleaf plantation on ancient woodland site - beech and sycamore replacing oak-ash-hazel stands
4   Conifer plantations on ancient woodland sites
5   Recent semi-natural broadleaf woodland - birch invading old grassland
6   Recent "semi-natural" conifer (pine) stand on raised bog
7   Recent broadleaf plantations - amenity plantations in old parkland
8   Recent conifer plantation on hill land

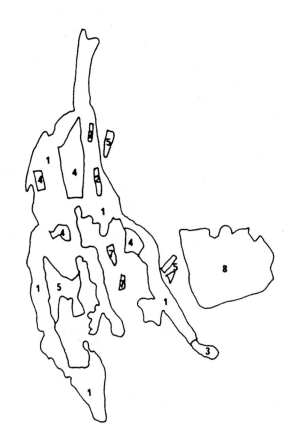

1km

N

Habitat mapping

Another form of Level 1 survey is represented by habitat mapping projects, often carried out on a field-by-field basis, which include some information about any woods encountered. This system has been adopted for the habitat mapping of SSSIs which is done as part of the renotification exercise. Details of the methods are given by Walton (1985).

(a)   Figure 3   Habitat map

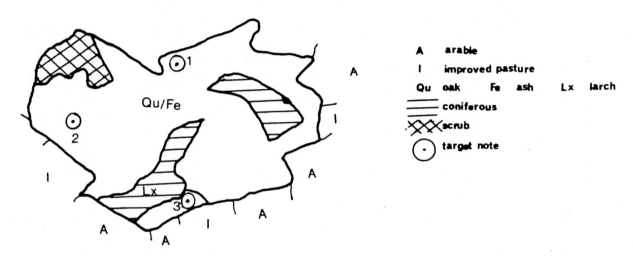

(b)   Key to habitat mapping categories for woodland

Habitat division				Colour used (Berol pencils)	Other details
1 Woodland	1	Broadleaf	1 Semi-natural	Green (solid)	Dominant species coded
			2 Plantation	Green (hatched)	
	2	Coniferous	1 Semi-natural	True green (solid)	
			2 Plantation	True green (hatched)	
	3	Mixed	1 Semi-natural	True green blobs on green	
			2 Plantation	True green/ green cross-hatch	

2 Scrub   )

3 Parkland/scattered trees   )   Equivalent colour codes and symbols

4 Recently felled woodland   )

(c)   Target notes ⊙ are used to provide a little more information about the composition of the areas shown on the map or features of interest.

1   Worked coppice with standards, <u>Quercus</u> <u>robur</u> over <u>Corylus</u> <u>avellana</u>, bracken <u>Pteridium</u> <u>aquilinum</u>, <u>Melampyrum</u> <u>pratense</u>, <u>Holcus</u> <u>mollis</u>.

2   Wide open ride; flowering edges potentially good for butterflies.

3   Blocks of conifers within wood, mainly 30-40 yr old larch, but with some 10-15 yr old spruce.

Canopy cover surveys

In upland Britain, where woodlands tend to occur mainly along valley sides and where the range of native woodland trees is limited, surveys based on the appearance of the canopy from a distance can be useful. Such surveys have been carried out in the Yorkshire Dales and Lake District National Parks (Bunce & Bunce 1977; LDSPB 1978) and in Scotland (Bunce, Munro & Parr 1979; Parr 1981) (Table 2; Figure 4). Forestry Commission stock maps may be used in a similar way (Figure 5).

Table 2   Results from a canopy survey of Scottish deciduous woodland (Bunce, Munro & Parr 1979; reproduced by permission of ITE)

Part of the inventory of deciduous woods in Scotland, with specific reference to tree species groups forming more than 1% of canopy (Parr 1981)

Species codings are: SY = sycamore, EL = elm, BE = beech, AS = ash, EX = exotics, LI = lime, SP = Scots pine, OA = oak, CH = cherry, HA = hawthorn, WI = willow, AL = alder, HZ = hazel, AP = aspen, RO = rowan, BI = birch. Contributions of holly, hornbeam, blackthorn, whitebeam and yew to woodland canopies never exceeded 1%.

County	Areas of deciduous woodland (ha)	Areas of woodland as % of area of county	SY	EL	BE	AS	EX	LI	SP	OA	CH	HA	WI	AL	HZ	AP	RO	BI
Sutherland	2900	0.6	1	0	1	1	3	0	2	4	0	0	2	6	2	-	3	74
Caithness	500	0.3	14	5	15	9	8	0	1	0	0	0	0	1	1	1	2	43
Ross	4020	0.6	1	0	4	1	4	0	7	9	0	0	1	2	2	0	2	67
Inverness*	10100	0.9	0	0	1	2	4	0	9	12	0	0	0	2	1	0	1	68
Nairn	630	1.6	1	0	11	6	10	0	2	8	0	0	0	0	0	0	0	62
Moray	1910	0.8	1	0	5	0	9	0	1	3	0	0	0	3	3	0	0	81
Banff	1250	0.6	4	2	9	5	14	1	11	5	0	0	0	3	3	0	1	45
Aberdeen*	2860	0.4	3	1	10	3	12	0	2	5	0	0	1	3	0	0	0	60
Kincardine*	440	0.6	3	3	9	3	7	0	5	4	0	0	2	1	0	0	1	62
Angus*	1360	1.3	3	4	23	3	9	0	4	8	0	0	2	1	2	0	0	43
Argyll	10190	1.1	3	1	4	4	6	0	1	36	0	0	0	2	0	0	1	39
Perth	7230	2.5	2	3	7	4	13	0	2	23	0	0	1	2	2	0	0	44
Stirling*	2960	1.4	10	4	8	5	7	0	1	31	0	0	0	2	0	0	0	30
Kinross	300	2.3	4	2	15	2	6	1	2	5	0	0	1	0	0	0	0	64
Dunbarton	1440	2.0	7	1	5	5	5	0	1	41	0	0	0	4	1	0	0	28
Clackmannan	280	1.1	7	6	12	10	13	0	3	5	0	0	0	4	0	0	0	39
Fife*	1400	1.3	16	9	14	7	11	1	2	9	0	0	1	1	0	0	0	29
Renfrew	770	1.2	21	4	19	8	7	2	1	8	0	0	1	7	1	0	0	29
Bute*	670	0.8	5	1	15	4	6	1	1	10	0	0	1	1	0	0	0	47
Ayr	2480	1.0	11	5	16	12	8	3	1	12	0	0	3	3	1	0	0	28
Lanark	2390	1.1	11	7	17	7	9	3	3	8	0	1	3	2	0	0	0	29
West Lothian	350	1.5	15	19	14	6	9	3	3	14	1	0	2	0	0	0	0	13
Midlothian	1410	1.5	14	10	18	9	21	1	3	13	0	0	0	0	0	0	0	11
East Lothian	1030	1.5	15	8	12	11	15	3	8	13	0	0	0	0	0	0	0	15
Peebles	350	0.4	6	7	17	8	18	2	12	7	0	0	1	0	0	0	0	19
Berwick*	920	0.8	18	6	17	6	9	1	4	19	0	0	0	1	2	0	0	20
Selkirk	130	0.2	5	11	9	21	15	1	2	21	1	0	0	0	0	0	0	14
Roxburgh*	730	0.4	10	12	17	7	13	1	4	25	1	0	3	1	0	0	1	9
Wigtown	1180	0.9	17	5	18	10	10	0	1	14	0	0	3	3	0	0	0	18
Kirkcudbright	1860	0.8	8	2	9	8	5	0	0	37	0	0	2	2	0	0	0	27
Dumfries	1990	0.7	5	3	14	10	7	0	1	30	0	0	0	3	0	0	0	27
Total	66030																	
Means		0.9	5	3	8	5	8	0	3	18	0	0	1	2	1	0	1	45

Asterisks indicate that surveys were less than 98% complete.

Results from a canopy survey of Scottish deciduous woodland

Figure 4   Area of birch woodland per 10 km square derived from the same data as
Table 2   (Kirby 1984a: reproduced from <u>Transactions of the Botanical
Society of Edinburgh</u> by permission of the editors)

■ less than 11 ha;   ● 11-100 ha;   ▼ more than 100 ha

a   Woods where birch forms more than 75% of the canopy

b   Woods where birch forms 25-75% of the canopy

Figure 5   Forestry   Commission   surveys   and   censuses   (Crown   copyright,
reproduced by permission of the Forestry Commission)

(a)   Part of a stock map showing the usual information recorded

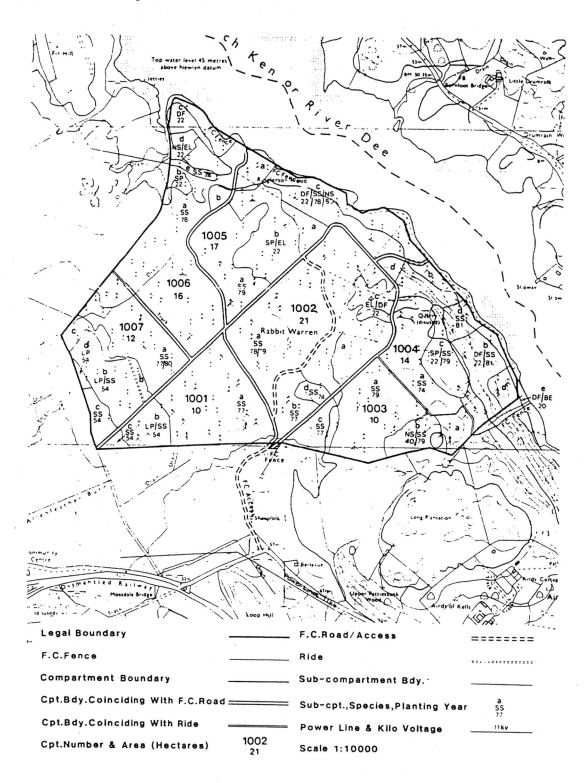

Legal Boundary	————————	F.C.Road/Access	========
F.C.Fence	————————	Ride	···.···········
Compartment Boundary	————————	Sub-compartment Bdy.	————————
Cpt.Bdy.Coinciding With F.C.Road	════════	Sub-cpt.,Species,Planting Year	a SS 77
Cpt.Bdy.Coinciding With Ride	════════	Power Line & Kilo Voltage	11kv
Cpt.Number & Area (Hectares)	1002 21	Scale 1:10000	

(b)   An extract from a 1947 census record showing part of the map, species and
structural data recorded

SUMMARY STATEMENT OF SPECIES

SPECIES STANDARDS	PER CENT (BY CANOPY)*	SPECIES COPPICE	PER CENT (BY CANOPY)*
OAK	90	S.CHESTNUT	90
S.P.		HAZEL	10
S.CHESTNUT	10	ALDER	
BEECH			
C.P.			

*Or by number of stems in young crops where the canopy has not closed.

CENSUS OF WOODLANDS, 1947-1949

(1)	COUNTY	KENT		MAP NO.	45 NE	STAND NO.	64	AREA: Acres gross	21
(2)	SURVEYOR.NO.ITLS DATE	39.JPW.16·6·49	CODE NO. 86	CODE NO.	45–2	CODE NO.	64	PRIVATE ⊠ FOR. COM.	2
(3)	NAME OF F.C. FOREST			CODE NO.		COMPT. NO.		CODE NO.	
(4)	TYPE	C.H.F. 1	M.H.F. 2	B.H.F. 3	COPP. W.STD ⊠ 4	COPP. 5	SCRUB 6	DEVST. 7	FELLED 8	LOST 9
(5)	AGE CLASS	1/10 1	11/20 2	21/30 3	31/40 4	41/60 5	61/80 6	81/120 7	OVER 120 8	UNEVEN 9
(6)	SUB-TYPE	CHEST COPP ⊠ 1	HAZEL COPP. 2	OAK COPP. 3	OTHER COPP. 4	UNEVEN AGED UND PL NT REG 5	PL NT REG 6	BEFORE 8/39 7	AFTER 8/39 8
(7)	TREE FORM	ELITE FOR SEED ⊠ 1	SATIS. 2	POOR 3	BAD 4	STOCK-ING	BADLY OVER STOCKED ⊠ 1	SATIS. 2	POOR 3	BAD 4
(8)	SUITABILITY for ECONOMIC MANAGEMENT	SUIT-ABLE ⊠ 1	DOUBT-FUL 2	UNSUIT-ABLE 3					

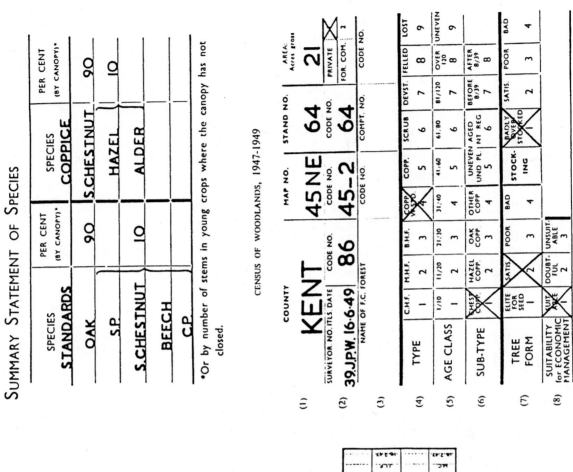

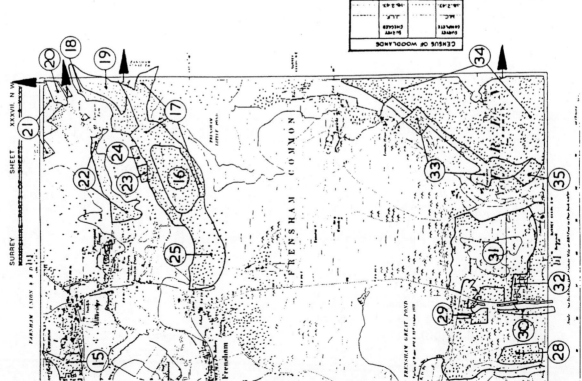

Forestry Commission censuses

The censuses carried out by the Forestry Commission correspond to Level 1 surveys as far as nature conservation value is concerned. The 1947 census attempted complete site-by-site coverage and the original data sheets from this are now available from the Public Record Office (Figure 5b). There is great potential for using these to study woodland change at a local level, although a complication is that many of the sites in 1947 had been devastated (felled or very heavily thinned) during the war. Subsequent censuses have been based on samples of woods and much of the basic data is still treated as confidential under the 30 year rule. Hence only statistics at the county or district level upwards are readily available (Table 3) (Locke 1970, 1987; Watkins 1984). These census results can be used to put "partial" woodland surveys into context.

Table 3   Part of the county results from the Forestry Commission's 1979-82 census (FC 1983) (Crown copyright, reproduced by permission of the Forestry Commission)

Area (hectares) of woodland by forest type and ownership in Hertfordshire

Forest type	Forestry Commission area	% of total	Dedicated and approved area	% of total	"Other" area	% of total	Total area	% of total
Mainly coniferous high forest	438	52	1307	37	471	6	2216+	18
Mainly broadleaved high forest	410	48	1893	54	5031*	63	7334+	59
Total high forest	848	100	3200	91	5502	69	9550+	77
Coppice with standards	-	-	101	3	88	1	189	2
Coppice	-	-	45	1	312	4	357	3
Scrub	3	<1	95	3	1390	17	1488+	12
Cleared	1	<1	83	2	702	9	786	6
Total	852	100	3524	100	7994	100	12370	100

* This figure for mainly broadleaved high forest contains 2.1 per cent of coppice origin.

+ Standard errors on the area estimates of forest types are as follows:

Mainly coniferous high forest	± 7.7 per cent
Mainly broadleaved high forest	± 5.4 per cent
Total high forest	± 4.2 per cent
Scrub	± 20.0 per cent

The percentage standard errors of area estimates of the remaining forest types are higher than these.

Other surveys

Large-scale O. S. maps can provide much detail (Harley 1975, 1979). The two Land Use Surveys (Stamp 1948, 1950, 1962; Coleman & Shaw 1980; Balchin 1985) can be useful for assessing land-use change (including woodland), as may earlier surveys of this type, for example those of Smith (1900) and Smith (1904). Another approach is to use "land classes" as a basis for strict stratified random sampling (Bunce, Barr & Whittaker 1983). Assessments of habitat change from air photographs (Langdale-Brown 1980) form the basis for the NCC's National Countryside Monitoring Scheme.

Use of Level 1 surveys

Level 1 survey results may be used to plan more detailed woodland surveys, for example to identify for future survey ancient semi-natural sites of more than 5 ha. Blocks of woodland which had hitherto escaped attention because they are relatively inaccessible may be identified. Even so, there may be too many sites to consider surveying them all. Depending on the objectives, a representative sample for surveying may be chosen (e.g. Highland Regional Council 1985), or other factors such as size may be used to concentrate the survey on the sites most likely to be valuable.

Patterns of woodland distribution in relation to geology, past land-use or topography often emerge more obviously from this type of survey than from more detailed surveys which (almost inevitably) cover fewer sites (Figure 6). Equally, the results may help to put a site into a broader context, e.g. to show that it is the sixth largest broadleaf woodland in the county.

From a comparison of surveys, statistics may be obtained on the total amounts of woodland in different categories and how these are changing, though difficulties arise where the categories used are not exactly compatible (Everett 1984; Peterken & Allison in prep.; Watkins 1985).

Conclusions

In most counties or districts there is already much information available and Level 1 surveys for woodland can be seen principally as a mechanism for drawing together as much of this as possible (Table 4). It is an area where the recent improvement of remote sensing techniques is likely to have a major impact (e.g. Fuller 1983; Goossens, van Genderen & De Wulf 1984).

Figure 6   Woodland distribution patterns at a county level (from Kirby et al. 1984)

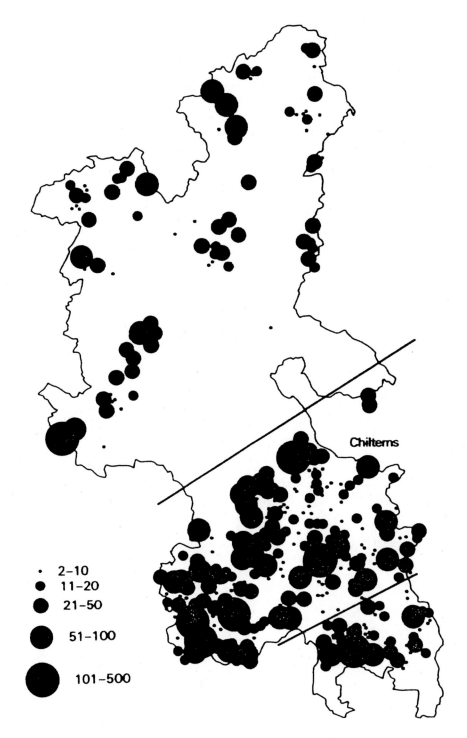

The distribution of ancient woodland in Buckinghamshire shows very distinct patterns, with relatively few such woods surviving in the clay vale (which has good agricultural soils) in the north of the county except on a few large private estates or in the remnants of the former royal hunting forests. By contrast, large areas of ancient woodland survive in the Chilterns (mainly on steep slopes) and on the poor acid soils to the south.

Table 4   Some sources of information on woodlands at a county level

(a)   Nature Conservancy Council

Ancient Woodland Inventories
Other surveys
SSSI schedules
Aerial photographs (usually limited)

(b)   County and District Councils

Structure plans, local plans and supporting documents
Aerial photographs

(d)   Parish Councils

Local advice and ownerships

(e)   Libraries and record offices

Old Ordnance Survey maps
Other historical material (e.g. tithe maps and local historical society reports)
County floras (which may refer to particular sites)
General county descriptions
The Victoria County History series

(f)   Forestry Commission offices

Stock maps for its own properties
Census information
Ownership

(g)   Voluntary conservation bodies

Surveys
Local knowledge of sites

(h)   Other organisations (NFU, CLA, TGUK etc)

Help and advice (through their members) on attitudes towards woodlands, how
they are managed, access for surveys, etc

(i)   Published papers, e.g. the descriptive studies in Journal of Ecology prior to
1940 (e.g. Watt 1925; Salisbury 1916)

This is not intended as a complete list, merely as a starting point.

Site surveys (Level 2) – general points

Introduction

Level 2 surveys are based upon a site visit of (usually) between three and six hours for a site of about 30–50 ha. The field records may take various forms, from handwritten notes to prepared forms with boxes to be ticked or species to be crossed off. In the future there may be direct input to portable computer terminals as in the most recent Forestry Commission census. Records may refer to the whole site or to representative sample areas within the wood; maps as well as lists or written descriptions may be involved. Whatever form it takes, the record provides the basis for the description and the preliminary classification and evaluation of the site (Figure 7).

Figure 7   Output from a Level 2 survey

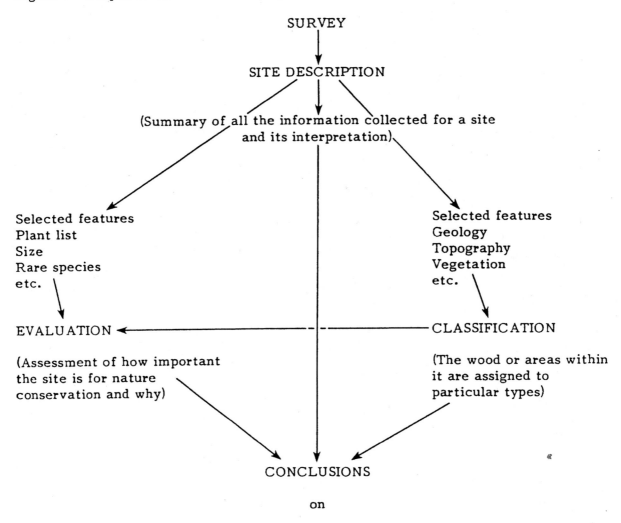

The description is the primary product of the survey and is the sum total of all that is recorded about the wood. In contrast, only part of the record may be used in the evaluation or in the classification; the latter in particular is often based on relatively few attributes. For example, the nature of the wood boundary and of the transition to adjacent land is an important part of the description and it sometimes forms part of evaluation schemes, but only the plant list might be used in woodland classification.

Classification is the process by which woods are grouped according to their possession of similar attributes. Plant communities are the main basis for classification, but other features such as geology, structure or situation are equally useful in particular circumstances. If types (however defined) can be recognised in the field, they may form part of the descriptive process, e.g. "north-east corner of wood is type X, remainder of site is type Y".

Evaluation involves the "measurement" of particular features which are used to indicate the nature conservation value of a site, for example how many plant species it contains. Sites identified as similar through the classification may be compared, and from this an assessment can be made that the site is perhaps of SSSI standard or that further survey is required to check on a particular feature or that a certain treatment is required to maintain or increase the site's value for nature conservation.

What do you record?

The following elements feature in most of the woodland surveys for nature conservation carried out over the last 10 years:

(a)   a map showing the location, extent and shape of the wood and the main internal features (glades, streams, major variations in vegetation, etc);

(b)   a list of the vascular plant species present with some indication of the relative abundance of different species;

(c)   an indication of the woodland structure;

(d)   a list of the "subsidiary habitats" present, such as streams, glades or cliffs;

(e)   a note on the adjacent land and the boundary of the wood; (The nature of the boundary should be marked on the map.)

(f)   the management of the wood, including signs of disturbance or the presence of introduced species;

(g)   the vegetation types present and an indication of their distribution, preferably with their boundaries clearly marked on the map;

(h)   a note on any rare species known to be present, with their locations marked;

(i)   some assessment of the value of the wood for other species groups - bryophytes, lichens, fungi, birds, mammals, invertebrates;

As Table 5 shows, these elements are related to the criteria for assessing nature conservation sites that are listed by Ratcliffe (1977).

Although components of a general site description have been listed above, there are still many different ways in which these might be recorded. For example, should the surveyors attempt to list all the plant species in a wood or concentrate on those associated with the "woodland" environment and ignore those found only on rides?

Should the plant list be produced from a walk through the site or from a series of quadrats placed in the wood? If the latter method is adopted, how many quadrats should be used, what size should they be, how distributed, and so on?

There are limits to what can be recorded in a short survey: rare species are very likely to be missed; the management and structure can be described only in fairly simple terms. Possibly the most important single feature is the vascular plant list, incomplete though it will be. The plants reflect the environmental conditions and history of the site, and they provide the food or living space for many of the other groups of species. They are relatively easy to record, compared with invertebrates for example, so that it is easier to get comparable results from different sites, even with inexperienced surveyors.

There is probably no single best method which is appropriate for all conditions, although those outlined in Appendix 3 have proved flexible enough to cope with most circumstances. They are therefore recommended as a basis for Level 2 surveys. The background to their use is contained in the following sections on different elements of woodland survey. These sections can also be used for planning more detailed study (Level 3 surveys).

Table 5   Criteria for judging nature conservation value (Ratcliffe 1977) and their relationship to commonly recorded woodland features

Nature Conservation Review criteria	Field measures
Size	Extent
Diversity	Plant list, structure, presence of subsidiary habitats and adjacent land, range of vegetation types, range of other species groups present
Naturalness	Lack of management, some types of woodland structure, some vegetation patterns, lack of introduced species
Rarity	Presence of any rare species or features
Place in ecological/ geographical unit	Location and nature of adjacent land, relation to the regional woodland pattern
Fragility	Some types of woodland are believed to be more "fragile" (sensitive to disturbance/non-recreatable if disturbed) than others. These should be recognisable from the general site description.
Representativeness	This can be judged by vegetation types, structure, location, topography, etc.
Recorded history	Often picked up in Level 1 surveys or preparatory work for Level 2 survey. Historical features may also be noted in the field.
Intrinsic appeal	This can only be judged once someone has visited the site.
Potential value	This can be judged in part from the management.

Vascular plant recording in woodlands

Plant parameters (Figure 8)

From a nature conservation viewpoint the most useful "plant parameters" to know for a wood are:

(a)   a list of the species present,

(b)   some measure of their abundance,

(c)   the distribution of particular species or groups of species,

(d)   the location and relative abundance of the vegetation types present.

This section is mainly concerned with (a) and (b); the other parameters are considered in the sections on mapping and classification. Estimates of the mean number of species per unit area are little used in woodland nature conservation work, unlike in grassland studies (Smith, Wells & Welsh 1985).

Sampling methods

General accounts of species and vegetation sampling and analysis dealing with the use of quadrats, transects, point-sampling and so on can be found in Greig-Smith (1983), Kershaw (1973), Muller-Dombois & Ellenberg (1974) and Moore & Chapman (1986). In practice, in most nature conservation surveys either the surveyor records the species seen during a walk through the wood (often called the "walkabout" method), or he/she lists the species found in a series of quadrats scattered through the wood. A third option is to combine the two approaches, with a list from the walk being supplemented by the species found in a few quadrats.

Other aspects of the woodland such as structure and management must be recorded at the same time as the plant species list. Therefore decisions on which survey method to adopt for plant recording cannot be divorced from consideration of how appropriate it is for assessing the structure of or for classifying the wood. The general conclusion, which applies to recording other features as well as the plants, is that the effectiveness and efficiency of the "walkabout" method increases relative to the use of quadrats as the resources, especially time, available for the survey are reduced (Figure 9).

Species listing on walks

A record of the species seen on a walk through a wood is effectively the record of a transect of varying width whose length depends on the time spent walking. The effective width of the transect is probably 2-3 m either side of the line of travel for most species, but it is greater for large conspicuous species such as foxgloves and less for inconspicuous plants such as herb-Paris among dog's mercury. The effective width is also greater in open low-growing communities than in tall bracken or bramble.

Where there is no previous knowledge of a site and the object is a plant record which can be compared with that from other sites, then the best route is one that covers the site in a more-or-less even manner. In practical terms this may mean walking round the edges of the wood and then making a series of forays into the centre in flat sites, or zigzagging up and down the slopes in hillside woods, or going up one side of the stream and down the other in long narrow valley woods (Figure 10). Where possible, the line should cut across any obvious source of variation such as the slope. In lowland woods the temptation to stick to rides and easy paths avoiding brambles must be countered.

Figure 8   Various "plant parameters" for a wood

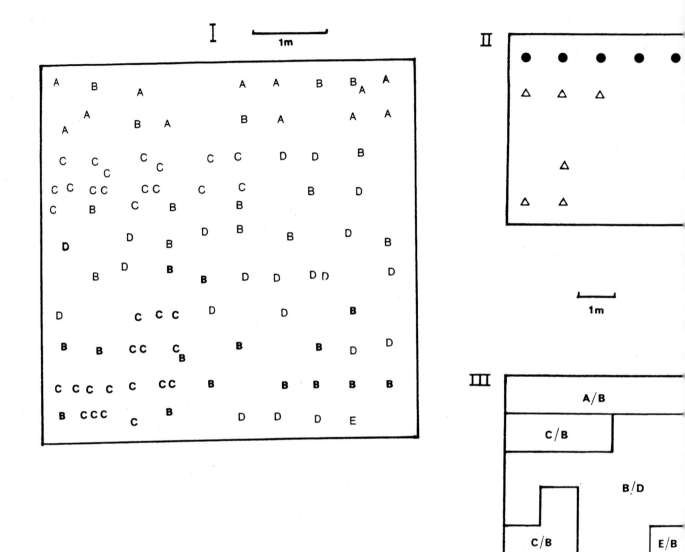

I   Each letter represents an individual plant of species A, B, etc in a fragment of Fangorn Forest.

The plant list for this section of forest consists of five species (A, B, C, D, E).
The mean density of plants (all species) is 4 per m² or (for species B) 1.25 per m².
The mean density of species is 2 per m².
With a 1 m² quadrat the frequency of occurrence of A is 20%, of B 100% and of E 4%, but all would show a frequency of 100% if a 5 x 5 m quadrat were used.

II   Distribution map for selected species for the same area (●) = A, (△) = B

III   Vegetation types for the same area

Figure 9   The relationship between the time spent recording and the number of species found on a walk and in quadrat surveys (Kirby et al. 1986: reproduced from Journal of Ecology by permission of the editors)

(a)   The accumulation of species with increased recording time as successive walks and sets of quadrats (mean recording time of 45 minutes per 200 m² quadrat assumed) are combined (∇ observer F, quadrats, Wytham Wood; ▲ observer E, walks, Wytham Wood; △ observer F, walks, Wytham Wood; ■ observer A, walks, Coedydd Aber)

(b)   The accumulation of species during the course of a walk in April (●) or May (O)

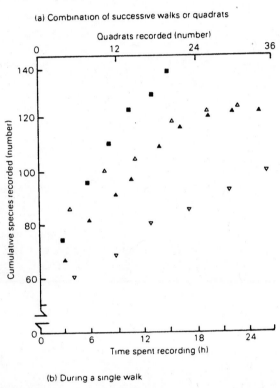

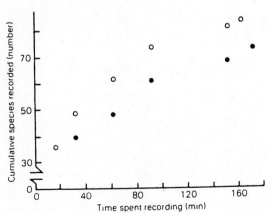

Figure 10   Possible survey routes in woodland

(a)   Flat, fairly uniform wood
(b)   Long, narrow hillside wood
(c)   Narrow valley woodland with stream in the bottom

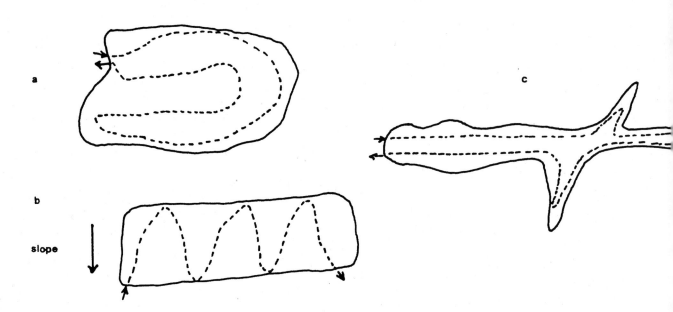

Table 6   Number of species detected on six walks through a wood when the length of
route remained the same in each case but the actual path followed varied
each time (Kirby et al. 1986: reproduced from Journal of Ecology by
permission of the editors)

	April/May Observers			August/September Observers	
	E	F		E	F
Number of species	67	86		80	88
found on each walk	72	93		86	89
	75	86		83	78
Mean:	71.3*	88.3	Mean:	83	85

Additional records by E

April	70
May	91
June	85
October	70

Each walk was approximately 3.0–3.5 km long and took between 2½ and 4 hrs. The wood
covered approximately 30 ha and the total species list for all records combined was
over 140 species.

*These records were made 2–3 weeks earlier than those by F and the difference
between the two sets of values is almost certainly caused by this.

It may be helpful to give surveyors a predetermined route marked on a map. Insistence on very strict adherence to such a route is, however, undesirable since, apart from the safety aspect, the surveyor wastes time checking that he/she is still on the route and the flexibility to investigate features which are just off the route is lost. Surveyors should mark the route taken on a map, particularly in large woods where the survey is likely to be incomplete. It is very easy to become disorientated in dense woodland, so use of a compass is strongly recommended. Taking aerial photographs showing woodland features into the field may help.

The number of species recorded varies with the time (distance) walked, but different routes of similar length tend to produce the same number of species (Table 6; Figure 9). The individual species recorded on different routes may not all be the same because, as with quadrat sampling, only a proportion of the total species complement is recorded.

Clearly, more species can be recorded in a given time if the surveyor already knows which areas are likely to contain "new" species and deliberately seeks these out, ignoring areas of the wood which appear to be relatively uniform. This leads to a much more rapid rise in the species accumulation/time graph. The greater the time available to spend on the survey, the smaller the difference between the number of species found on a walk deliberately designed to visit the richest areas and a route which covers the site evenly. Since, almost by definition, relatively little is known about the sites chosen for this level of survey, the use of routes which cover the site in a more-or-less even fashion is recommended.

Use of the DAFOR scale for species abundance assessment

At the end of the walk the abundance of each species seen can be assessed on a five-point scale - D = dominant, A = abundant, F = frequent, O = occasional, R = rare. These terms have no precise definition and observers vary in their use; both frequency of individuals and cover are combined (or confounded) in the one value and plant size and season affect the result. Nevertheless, these estimates are worth making, since they take only a few minutes and there is a broad correlation between them and more quantitative measures (Table 7). Most of the species found in 25-35 quadrats were scored as frequent or abundant, species found in 7-18 quadrats were mainly scored as occasional, while most species scored as rare either were not recorded at all or were recorded only in 1-6 quadrats.

Table 7 Comparison of subjective cover estimates with frequency data from quadrat surveys

DAFOR estimates of abundance for species seen on a three-hour walk through a wood compared with the frequency of occurrence for those species in 36 randomly placed 200 m^2 quadrats (from surveys described in Kirby et al. 1986)

DAFOR rating	No. of species					
Abundant (A)						4
Frequent (F)			3	3	4	5
Occasional (O)		7	9	6	4	1
Rare (R)	14	25		1		
	0	1-6	7-12	13-18	19-24	25-36

Frequency of occurrence in quadrats (out of 36)

Species listing from quadrats - number and size of quadrat

A quadrat sample covers a smaller total area in the same time than is considered by a walk transect. Hence the species list produced is shorter. In addition, if only quadrats are recorded, the time spent walking between positions is largely wasted. However the ground within the quadrats is examined in more detail than any point on the walk route so that the less conspicuous species are more likely to be identified. The species records are also more-or-less precisely located. The main factors which determine the number of species found in a set of quadrats are:

(a)   the size of the quadrat,

(b)   the number of quadrats recorded,

(c)   the distribution of the quadrats.

The relationships between quadrat size, quadrat number and the number of species detected in British woodlands have been thoroughly examined by Sykes & Horrill (1979) (Table 8; Figure 11). In practice the size of quadrat used is usually determined by the classification system that is employed (see later section). Most woodland survey work within NCC over the last five years has used a 200 m² (14.1 m x 14.1 m) quadrat, details of which are given in Appendix 3.

Past experience with the 200 m² quadrat suggests that the surveyor cannot record more than about 6 -12 a day, less if notes are made on species seen and the state of the wood between quadrat positions. There is therefore usually a low sampling percentage in woods surveyed in this way (Table 9).

If, in future surveys, the quadrat data are only required to help classify stands by the National Vegetation Classification System then a shift to separate ground flora (4 x 4 m or 10 x 10 m) and tree and shrub layer quadrats (50 x 50 m) is recommended (see Appendix 2). If a combined record of tree, shrub and ground flora layers is required, the 200 m² quadrats is preferable.

Random, systematic, stratified random and subjective plot positions

The number of species and the amount of variation in, for example, vegetation types depends on how the quadrats are positioned in the wood.

Four types of quadrat distribution may be used in woodland surveys:

(a)	random	)	Within-site variation, even if known, is
		)	irrelevant to the distribution of the
(b)	systematic	)	plot positions.
(c)	stratified random	)	Within-site variation is used in determining
		)	the distribution of the plots.
(d)	subjective	)	

Random distribution

A random distribution means that there is an equal chance that any particular point in the wood may be assigned to a quadrat position. The simplest way to achieve a set of random positions is to cover a map of the site with a fine grid overlay and then assign quadrat positions to points on the grid using co-ordinates (as in a game of Battleships) derived from random number tables or a calculator. In the field the surveyor usually locates the quadrat position by pacing along a compass bearing from some well-defined point along a ride or the wood boundary. For most purposes it does not matter if the

Table 8   The relationship between quadrat size, quadrat number and the number of plant species detected (from Sykes & Horrill 1979: reproduced by permission of ITE)

No. of species occurring in different sizes of quadrat

Wood	No. of quadrats	Quadrat size (m²)				
		4	25	50	100	200
Colt Park	25	92	115	121	128	138
Hales	33	53	69	78	83	91
Meathop	76	68	98	113	127	136
Rodney	105	91	110	120	134	152
Glasdrum	71	116	135	146	152	158
Roudsea	80	122	157	172	190	205
Kirkconnell	159	50	64	73	81	82

Table 9   The sampling percentages achieved by varying numbers of 200 m² quadrats in woods of different sizes

No. of 200 m² quadrats per wood	Size of wood (ha)			
	2	5	20	50
	Sampling percentages			
2	2	0.8	0.2	0.08
4	4	1.6	0.4	0.16
8	8	3.2	0.8	0.32
16	16	6.4	1.6	0.64

Keeping the number of quadrats per wood fixed means that the same total area is sampled in each case; varying the number in relation to the size of the wood allows for a more constant sampling percentage. Both systems have disadvantages when it comes to extrapolating from the quadrat records to the condition and conservation value of the whole wood.

For comparison, each of the 3 km walk routes used in the 30 ha wood which provided the data for Table 6 is equivalent to a 4% sample if it is assumed that the effective width of the transect sampled is 4 m (2 m either side of the line of travel).

Figure 11   The relationship between the number of species found and the size and the number of quadrats recorded (from Sykes & Horrill 1979: reproduced by permission of the authors)

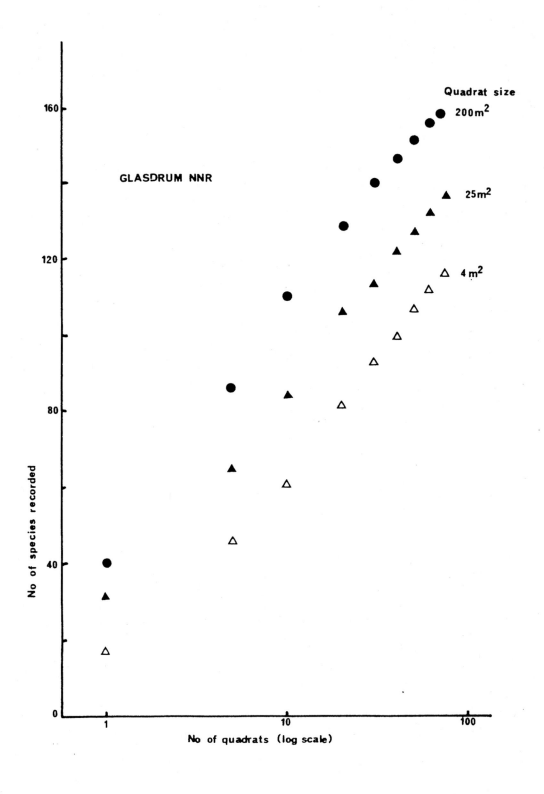

actual position of the quadrat is not quite where the original mark was on the map as long as the surveyor has not consciously or unconsciously biased the final position. Quadrats which fall across sharp vegetation boundaries or on rides or piles of logging waste must be accepted as a valid part of the survey (Bunce & Shaw 1973).

A random plot distribution has the advantage that it does not require any pre-existing knowledge of the variation within the site and, because the sites are predetermined, there is less risk of observer bias in their final positioning. However, random plot sampling is much less efficient for detecting the range of species or vegetation types within a wood than either systematic or stratified random sampling (Dawkins & Field 1978; Kirby 1984b). If the sets of quadrats are small (less than 10 quadrats per set), the high variation in the numbers of species found in sets taken from the same wood could be as great as the differences found between sets from different woods (Table 10).

The main use for small-scale random sampling in nature conservation surveys is not in general Level 2 site surveys, but in comparisons of the mean cover of vegetation layers, the mean numbers of species in different stands or the frequency with which a species occurs in a stand (Table 11).

Table 10   Variability in the total number of species recorded from small sets of quadrats (from surveys described by Kirby et al. 1986)

	No. of species found in three separate sets of six randomly placed quadrats				Total number (all results combined)
Wood A	73	71	36	mean 60	139
Wood B	62	60	57	mean 59.7	118

When all records are considered, Wood A is richer than Wood B, as is suggested by the results from the first two sets of quadrats. If only the third set of quadrat results were available (where by chance all the quadrats in A fell in species-poor areas), the conclusion would have been that A was much less species-rich than B.

Table 11   A comparison of different silvicultural treatments in Salcey Forest, based on 10 randomly placed quadrats in each treatment

Planting date Species	1847 oak	1905 oak	1945 oak:NS	1955 oak:NS	1977 oak:NS
Mean % cover per quadrat					
Tree layer	87	79	77	83	0
Shrub layer	50	51	16	7	2
Field layer	64	66	44	7	85
Mean no. of species per 200 m² plot	37.9	38.7	34.9	22.2	40.6
Frequency of species occurrence					
No. of species present in 9 or 10 plots	16	13	6	7	8
No. of species present in only 1 or 2 plots	27	30	24	24	40

NS = Norway spruce

Figure 12   Species distribution and cover based on a systematic sampling pattern (from Horsfall & Kirby 1985)

The survey was based on 10 x 10 m quadrats at alternate intersections of a 100 m grid. Species distributions for ash (a), sycamore (b) and field maple (c) are presented. △ relevant species present in the quadrats, ▲ present in the canopy and providing up to 50% of the cover; ■ providing more than 50% of the canopy cover.

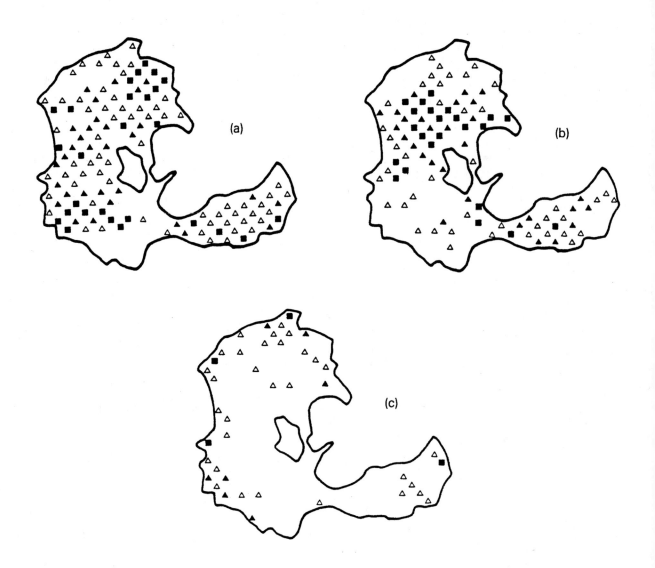

Systematic (grid) distribution

Systematic distributions of quadrat positions, usually based on a grid, are a very efficient way of detecting species or events, because once a vegetation type, for example, exceeds the grid size it must be detected (Dawkins & Field 1978). A systematic distribution prevents all the quadrat positions being at one end of a wood, as could happen with a random distribution. It is however possible for the spacing of the grid to coincide with some more-or-less systematic variation in the environment, so that a particular feature is either under- or over-represented. If the number of quadrats is small it may be difficult to devise a systematic distribution that does not tend to oversample the edge of the wood. Estimates of the frequency of species, the mean number of species per plot and the mean species cover can be calculated for a systematic layout, but the usual formulae for calculating standard errors and confidence limits (which assume a random distribution) should not be used. Systematic distributions of quadrats are very useful in distribution mapping studies (see, for example, Horrill, Sykes & Idle 1975 and Figure 12) and in monitoring work (see later), but they have only limited application in general Level 2 site surveys.

Stratified random quadrat distribution

In stratified random sampling the wood is divided into sections, or "strata", such that the variation within each stratum is less than that between them; i.e. a heterogeneous wood is divided into a series of strata each of which is more-or-less homogeneous. The quadrats are positioned at random within each stratum, with a minimum of two per stratum. The numbers of quadrats per stratum do not have to be equal or related to the area of the stratum, although interpretation of the results may be easier if one or the other applies. According to statistical theory the most efficient method is to relate the number of samples to the expected level of variation in that stratum (Snedecor & Cochran 1967). Features such as geology, altitude or management compartments can be used to divide the wood into strata prior to the survey. If the aim is to detect species and vegetation types, then the vegetation differences themselves (as in Figure 15b, for example) may provide the most effective stratification (Table 12). However, on a single visit to a wood it may be difficult to produce a map of strata, determine random positions within these and then record the quadrats, without introducing considerable observer bias. Areas near the boundaries of strata, for example, are likely to be undersampled. The method then tends towards the subjective (representative) sampling described below. However, if the opportunity and resources exist for ensuring that the mapping (walk records) and quadrat recording stages are properly designed, a stratified random approach is the most effective way of combining the two methods of woodland survey. See Smart & Grainger (1974) for further discussion of the use of stratified random sampling.

Subjective (representative) quadrat distribution

In this method the surveyors simply choose where to put the quadrats, usually in places that in their opinion are representative of the vegetation in that part of the wood. There is no statistical basis for extrapolating from such quadrat records to the rest of the wood. Therefore they have little value in estimating either the total number of species in a wood or the abundance of any species. Such plots are, however, very useful in the description and classification of woodland vegetation. Subjective representative sampling depends on the experience of the surveyor, but is often the most effective way of using a small number of quadrats, since almost inevitably there will be a large statistical error attached to small random, stratified random or systematic samples, so that most of the advantages of an unbiased sample are lost anyway.

Table 12   A comparison of unrestricted random and stratified random sampling for the detection of plot types and plant species (from Kirby 1984b: reproduced by permission of the Field Studies Council)

Sets of six quadrats were drawn from a block of 62 quadrats, either at random or after stratification into three strata with two samples taken per stratum at random.   This procedure was repeated 10 times.

	Stratified random sample	Unrestricted random sample
Mean number of types detected in 6 quadrats (n=10)	4.8 + 0.1 Difference significant using t-test at p=0.99 level	4.0 + 0.2
Number of types detected in all replicates combined	12	10
Mean number of species detected in 6 quadrats (n=10)	60.0 + 2.5 Difference significant using t-test at p=0.99 level	47.9 + 2.5
Number of species detected in all replicates combined	106	89

Number of plot types in the complete block of 62 quadrats = 12
Number of plant species in the complete block of 62 quadrats = 115

Estimates of species abundance based on quadrats

Quadrat results can be used to estimate the frequency of occurrence of a species in a set of quadrats and also its mean cover per quadrat.   This last may be complicated if cover has been estimated on a Domin scale rather than directly as percentage cover. Within-plot abundance values are not widely used in the evaluation of sites, but they may be helpful in the description and classification of areas and in detailed studies within woods (Figure 13).

Just as surveyors differ in their interpretation and use of the DAFOR scale on walks, so surveyors differ in their assessments of cover within a given plot.   Sykes, Horrill & Mountfort (1983) found that most surveyors had a tendency to underestimate the cover of some species and overestimate that of others, but individuals did not always show a consistent tendency across all species relative to the mean estimate made by the group. There is also a difference between species in their frequency as assessed by cover or by the presence of rootstocks, as one would expect from differing growth structures, so surveyors must be clear which measure is to be used, particularly with trees and shrubs which spread widely.   Different methods of assessing cover are compared by Floyd & Anderson (1987).

Figure 13   Use of Domin values to compare species abundance in different parts of a
wood

The Domin scale

10	=	91 – 100% cover	
9	=	76 – 90	"
8	=	51 – 75	"
7	=	34 – 50	"
6	=	26 – 33	"
5	=	11 – 25	"
4	=	4 – 10	"

Less than 4% cover
3   =   frequent
2   =   sparse
1   =   rare

Abundance of <u>Mercurialis perennis</u> in quadrats taken from adjacent ancient and recent woods, (a) Plegdon Wood (ancient) and (b) Lady Wood (recent)

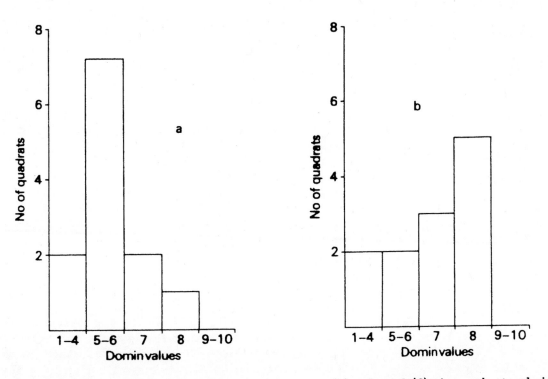

Abundance of <u>Luzula sylvatica</u> in quadrats taken from (c) oak and (d) pine-oak stands in Cawdor Wood (Nairn)

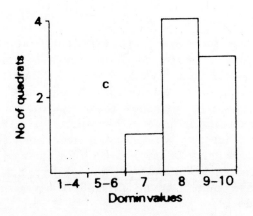
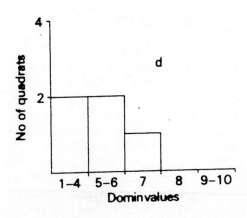

Walks or quadrats - which method?

If the main aim is to produce a list of species from a wood, there are good reasons for using a walk-based survey; more species are detected in a given time, the results are not significantly more variable than the most commonly used alternative, random quadrat samples (Kirby et al. 1986), and the DAFOR scale of abundance is likely to be sufficient for most purposes as an estimate of species abundance.

Quadrats are a valuable addition which can greatly improve vegetation description if the resources are available (Kirby 1982). There is a need to balance the time spent collecting information on the walk part of the survey with that spent recording plots. On short visits of less than a day the main emphasis should be on the walk; on longer ones there can be a shift to more quadrat recording.

The choice of which type of distribution pattern to use depends on how many quadrats there is time to record, whether estimates of species abundance and distribution are wanted, and whether the wood can be stratified in some way before locating the quadrats.

In summary:

Walk surveys:	the best method for obtaining an overall impression of a site in a short time.
Random samples:	useful for estimating species abundance in fairly uniform areas; inefficient for detecting species and vegetation types.
Systematic samples:	more efficient than random samples for detecting species; very useful in mapping and monitoring work.
Stratified random samples:	useful for describing previously mapped areas; some risk of observer bias being introduced; very effective as a sampling method.
Subjective representative samples:	their value depends entirely on the skill of the surveyor; they may be the most efficient way to use a small number of quadrats per site as an aid to vegetation description and classification. Note that the quadrat recording used in the National Vegetation Classification is based on this type of quadrat distribution. This classification may therefore be more difficult to use with random and systematic distributions and some stratified random patterns.

Other factors affecting species recording

Apart from the survey method, the factors most likely to affect the accuracy and completeness of any plant species record and estimates of plant cover within quadrats are the experience of observers and the time of year (Sykes, Horrill & Mountford 1983; Kirby et al. 1986; Kennedy & Addison 1987). Lists produced between late April and early September should be broadly comparable in terms of their length, though their precise composition varies (Table 13). If recording is done either earlier or later (and in spring it may be the difference of only one or two weeks' warm weather), the list of species found on a standard survey may show quite a large drop. Salisbury (1916) and Falinski (1986) illustrate the phenology of some woodland species, while Sykes & Horrill (1979) provide a preliminary list of species that may be missed or misidentified in surveys at different times of the year (Table 14).

Table 13 The effect of observer efficiency and season indicated by species in common between pairs of lists, expressed as a percentage of the number of species in the combined list (from Kirby et al. 1986: reproduced from Journal of Ecology by permission of the editors)

Site	Coedydd Aber	Wytham	Wytham	Glen Loin
Method	Walks	Walks	Quadrats	Quadrats
Records have: same observer, same season (12 values per site)	68.4 (61–75)	73.1 (60–80)	62.2 (52–74)	52.5 (40–64)
different observer, same season (18 values per site)	62.9 (56–69)	64.6 (53–76)	60.2 (56–66)	49.2 (38–60)
same observer, different season (18 values per site)	54.2 (48–61)	61.4 (53–70)	58.6 (52–68)	48.5 (36–58)
different observer, different season (18 values per site)	53.7 (50–60)	59.5 (51–65)	56.5 (51–68)	46.9 (32–55)

The figures show that, for instance, two lists produced in the same season by the same observer at Coedydd Aber using a "walk" method of recording had on average 68.4% of their species in common, whereas if both observer and season varied this figure was reduced to 53.7%. The mean values are given for all possible pairs of records in which either observer or season varies. Figures in brackets give the range of values found. Standard errors have not been calculated since the values obtained from different combinations are not independent of each other. The seasons were April/May and August/September.

Reasonably competent surveyors do not differ much in the length of the lists produced from a wood at a given time of year, although there may be discrepancies for closely related species pairs (e.g. Holcus lanatus, Holcus mollis; Rumex spp.) or for difficult groups such as sedges, roses and hawkweeds (Wigginton & Graham 1981). Initial training and good supervision during the survey should reduce these problems.

Less predictable are the effects of the weather, the steepness of slope, the number of midges and the height of the bracken or brambles. There is no question but that they reduce the morale and hence the efficiency of surveyors, as do complicated, unfamilar instructions and recording forms and heavy equipment such as quadrat poles. Pairs of surveyors working together help to maintain morale and to ensure consistent results and tend to increase the number of species recorded from a site in a given time. This increase in the quality of the result needs to be set against a net reduction in the rate of woodland recording, since two surveyors often do not work twice as fast as one. However, using pairs of surveyors is very desirable and sometimes essential for safety reasons.

Table 14   Species or genera which may be missed or misidentified in surveys (from Sykes & Horrill 1979: reproduced by permission of ITE)

State / Plant	Vanishes early (mid-July)	Residual floral parts or fruits	Identification difficult to species level	Flowers or fruit needed for identification	Morphological similarities to other plants	Flowers of short duration
Adoxa moschatellina	+					
Allium ursinum	+					
Anemone nemorosa	+					
Arum maculatum	+	+				
Alchemilla spp.			+			
Arctium spp.			+			
Betula spp.			+			
Conopodium majus	+	+				
Carex spp.			+	+		
Cirsium spp.			+	+		
Crepis spp.			+			
Endymion non-scriptus	+	+				
Epilobium spp.			+			
Euphrasia spp.			+		+	
Gagea lutea	+			+		
Galium spp.			+	+		
Gramineae (some)				+		
Hypericum spp.			+			
Hieracium spp.			+			
Juncus spp.			+	+		
Lathraea squamaria						+
Listera ovata	+		+			
Leontodon spp.			+			
Luzula spp.			+	+		
Mentha spp.			+	+		
Myosotis spp.			+	+		
Narcissus pseudonarcissus	+	+				
Neottia nidus-avis (+ other saprophytes)						+
Ophioglossum vulgatum					+	
Paris quadrifolia	+				+	
Poa spp.			+	+		
Populus spp.			+			
Quercus spp.			+			
Ranunculus ficaria	+					
Rosa spp.			+			
Rubus spp.			+			
Rumex spp.			+	+		
Salix spp.			+	+		
Sorbus spp.			+	+		
Taraxacum spp.			+			
Tilia spp.			+			
Ulmus spp.			+			
Viola spp.			+	+		

Year-to-year variations in survey results for a given wood may be expected where conditions are changing, for example where felling or coppicing occurs (Ash & Barkham 1976; Ford & Newbould 1977; Brown & Oosterhuis 1981), as previously open stands close canopy or as rides close over or are opened out. There may be smaller scale changes due to gains or losses of species by immigration and extinction (Woodroffe-Peacock 1918). Little work has been done on how this could effect comparisons between survey results taken from different years, but the results from the monitoring of permanent plots provide some indication of the level of variation that might occur. Falinski (1986) shows that the same species are not always recorded in permanent plots assessed in consecutive years although the variations are small. Similarly the species lists from 21 10 x 10 m plots recorded in 1974 and 1984 are very similar, and much of the variation can be ascribed to just three of the plots where it is believed that real changes in the ground flora had occurred (Table 15).

Table 15   Similarity of the ground flora (1974–1984) from 21 plots in Wytham Woods (Oxon) (from Horsfall & Kirby 1985)

(a)   No. of species recorded from all 21 plots in:

	1974	110
	1984	103
	both years	90

Sorensen's Similarity Index: 84%

(b)   Total number of species occurrences in:

	1974	459
	1984	399

Species occurrences common to both years: 334

Sorensen's Similarity Index (quantitative form):   78%

(c)   Mean number of species per plot ($\pm$S.E.) in:

	1974	21.8 ± 9.4 (n = 21)
	1984	18.7 ± 7.1 (n = 21)

Mean Sorensen's Similarity Index for an individual plot: $71.1 \pm 11.2\%$

The plots were 10 x 10 m and were precisely relocated in 1984. Real changes in the ground flora had almost certainly occurred in some plots.

Indicator species

Not all species are equally useful in assessing the nature conservation value of a site. More attention is paid to species associated with woodland habitats than to grassland or wetland species which occur in the wood because there is a large open ride or a pond. The work of Peterken (1974), Peterken & Game (1984), Pigott (1969) and Rackham (1980) suggests that there are plants which may be restricted to ancient woodland, at least in some counties. While it might save survey time to concentrate efforts on recording these "indicator" species and ignore more cosmopolitan ones, the consequent loss in information available for the description of the wood outweighs this possible advantage. Indicator species are more useful at the evaluation stage and a paper on the identification and use of indicator species is being prepared by Dr R J Hornby and Dr F Rose.

Mapping and classifying vegetation

Introduction

This section deals with the classification of woodland vegetation and the ways in which the distribution of individual species or of vegetation types may be mapped. Woods may also be mapped in terms of their canopy dominants or the age of the crop.

The classification of survey results may be approached in the following ways.

(a) The results collected in the survey are used to generate a classification specific to that set of data, a "local" classification, e.g. using computer packages such as ISA (Indicator Species Analysis: Hill, Bunce & Shaw 1975) or TWINSPAN (Hill 1979b).

(b) The results are collected in a way that enables them to be assigned to types within an existing classification system after the survey is complete.

(c) The surveyor classifies areas in the field, using an existing system.

Which approach is adopted depends on whether a satisfactory classification already exists and whether the types can be recognised in the field (Figure 15).

If a "local" classification is used, as in (a) above, this should be related to one (or more) of the existing national systems if it is to be more generally useful. If the classification is done in the field as in (c), sufficient detail should be recorded for at least a proportion of stands (a minimum of 10% is suggested) to confirm independently the surveyor's judgement.

Figure 14   Distribution maps

(a) Map based on extrapolation from a series of sample points with no information about the intervening areas

(b) Map of types produced during a walk through a wood

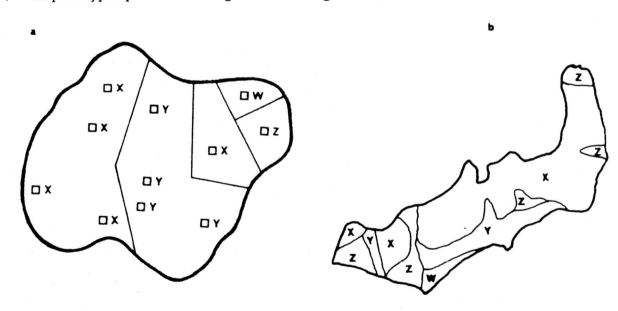

Figure 15   Different ways of approaching the classification problem

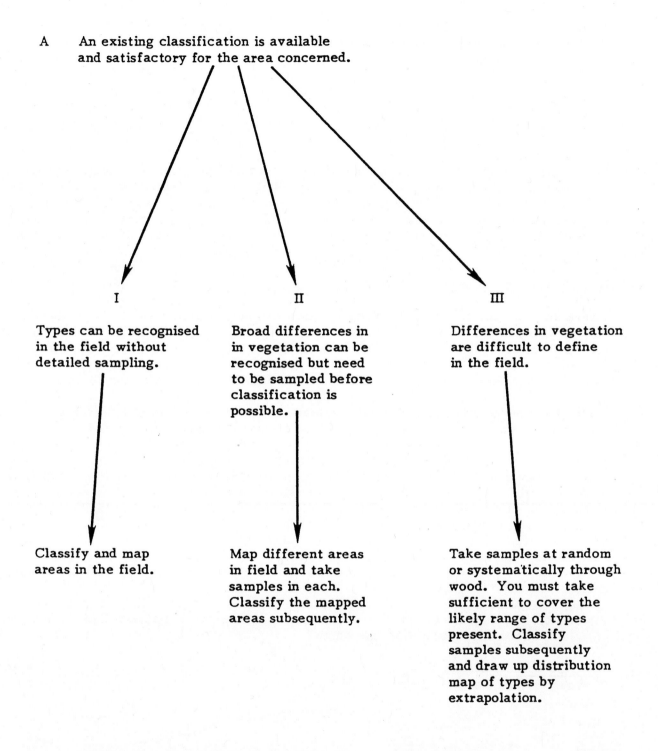

A   An existing classification is available
      and satisfactory for the area concerned.

I

Types can be recognised
in the field without
detailed sampling.

Classify and map
areas in the field.

II

Broad differences in
in vegetation can be
recognised but need
to be sampled before
classification is
possible.

Map different areas
in field and take
samples in each.
Classify the mapped
areas subsequently.

III

Differences in vegetation
are difficult to define
in the field.

Take samples at random
or systematically through
wood. You must take
sufficient to cover the
likely range of types
present. Classify
samples subsequently
and draw up distribution
map of types by
extrapolation.

B   Existing classifications are unavailable or inappropriate for the area concerned.
      Sample the area as in A II or A III, produce a local classification from the results
      and then proceed in further surveys as for A.

Classification and mapping

Most vegetation classifications are derived from the analysis of quadrat data. Thus quadrats recorded in the same way should be assignable, more or less unequivocally, to one or other type within the limits of the variation covered by the original survey. It is rarely practical to have 100% survey cover by quadrats in a wood and therefore it is useful if the areas between quadrat positions can also be assigned to a type. Either this is done in an arbitrary fashion - the type boundary between two quadrats of differing types being assumed to run halfway between their positions (Figure 14 (a)) - or the surveyor uses his or her judgement to determine where the boundary should run.

There is no a priori reason to assume that the quadrat positions are equidistant from type boundaries, particularly if the initial distribution was selected on a random basis. If there are only a few quadrat positions in a wood, additional types may be present but not recorded in the quadrats. If it is left to the surveyor's judgement, the boundary position may vary according to the skill of the surveyor and the distinctness of the types being separated. In many cases there is no distinct boundary between types but rather a zone where one grades into the other. Any attempt to represent this as a single boundary is a simplification.

Where the distinction between types is based on just a few features, "free mapping" may be used; in this case the surveyor assigns areas to types without the back-up of quadrat samples (Figure 14 (b)). This depends on the experience of the surveyor in being able to spot where a feature changes, altering the type. The Stand Type classification can (with experience) be used in this way, as can the National Vegetation Classification.

Where free mapping is used, quadrat samples should be taken at least during the early part of the survey to ensure consistent and accurate type identification. Further samples should be taken later in the survey to check that standards of identification are being maintained. A minimum of 10% of sites should be checked in this way. Free mapping may also be used to identify variation of a different type from or at a finer scale than that covered by the existing classification, to pinpoint particular features (Figure 16), or to describe variation in woods where existing classifications are inappropriate or inadequate, for example where tree dominants vary within a floristic type or where both high forest and coppice stands exist. Difficulties with free mapping may include problems in plotting precise boundaries on maps even if they are obvious on the ground and defining the minimum area that should be distinguished as a separate entity.

Figure 16   Mapping of individual features and small-scale variation within an area of comparatively uniform woodland

T = Tilia cordata stools; Y = yew groves; Bet = dense groves of young birch; Syc = areas of sycamore dominance; /// = clearings.

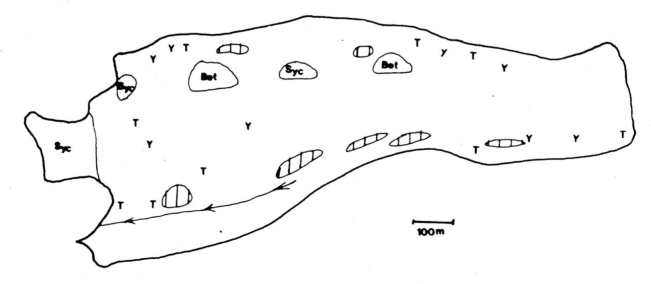

A distinction is sometimes drawn between maps produced by "free mapping", which are described as "complete", and those produced by extrapolation from a series of sample points, but however "complete" the map produced during a walk through a wood it almost always involves some extrapolation. This distinction is thus artificial and does not reflect a difference in the principles involved but a difference in the intensity of survey. The more evenly distributed the samples and the less the distance between them, the closer does a sample map approach the "true" picture - hence the great advantage of systematic distributions of quadrats over random ones for this purpose (Figures 17 and 18). The scale of the map used may also affect whether at a given level of survey intensity the resulting map is regarded as either "complete" or a sample: the larger the scale, the more space there is to show variation between sample points.

Figure 17 A hypothetical comparison of the results from free and sample point mapping (reproduced, by permission of the author, from Peterken 1981)

(a) The actual distribution of adult maple and hornbeam in a stand otherwise composed of ash, hazel and pedunculate oak. The stand measures 300 m x 450 m.

(b) The same stand divided into 150 squares of 30 m x 30 m, showing the Stand Type to which each square belongs. The Stand Types are 9Ab where the hornbeam is present, 2A where it is absent but maple is present, and 3A where neither hornbeam nor maple is present (see Appendix 4).

(c) A map of Stand Types as it might be prepared by a surveyor.

(d) A map of Stand Types prepared by sampling 25% of 30 m x 30 m squares, then interpolating Stand Type boundaries.

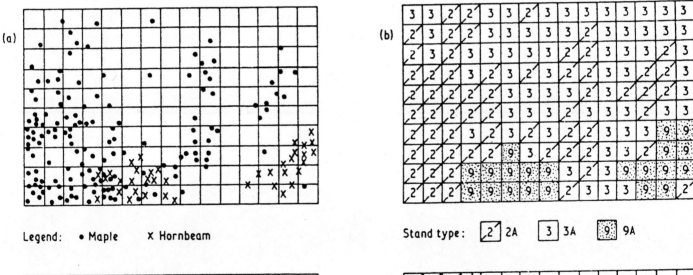

Legend: • Maple   x Hornbeam

Stand type: ⟨2⟩ 2A   ⟨3⟩ 3A   ⟨9⟩ 9A

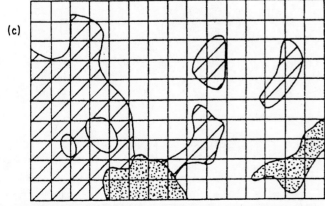

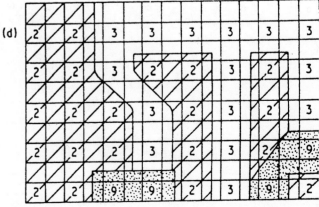

Figure 18   The effect of scale of sampling on distribution maps made by interpolation between sample points (Sykes 1981: reproduced by permission of ITE)

The upper map shows the distribution of types based on a grid sampling system with points every 100 m; the lower map shows the revised distribution of types produced when additional samples were added between the original points.

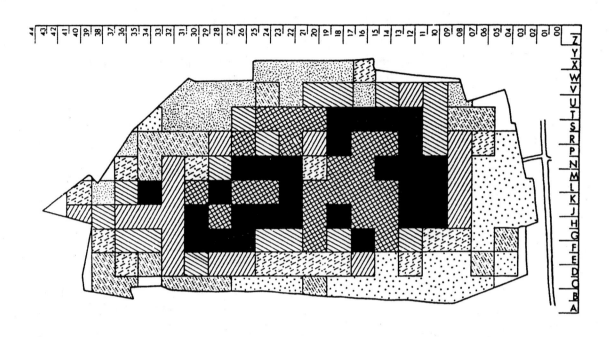

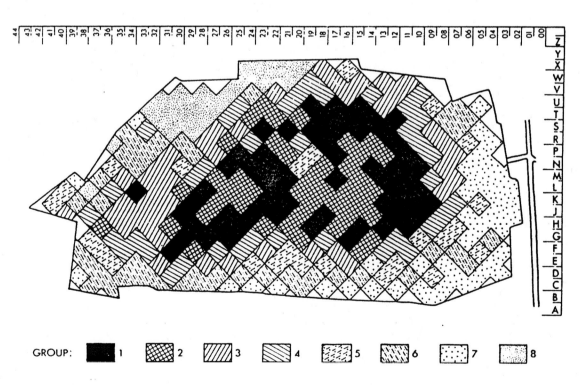

Free mapping produces the best approximation to the true distribution of vegetation types if the boundaries between types are easily recognisable, for example those between oak and alder stands, and the time for surveys is limited (as in many Level 2 surveys). Where the distinction between types is less clear-cut and more time is available, maps based on a large number of point samples become more useful.

The distribution of <u>rare</u> species or features, as opposed to the distribution of the main woodland types, usually requires "free mapping" combined with knowledge of the particular conditions under which that species or feature occurs; see for example the distribution of wood ant nests in Bedford Purlieus (Figure 19) found by searching relatively open sunny areas, mainly near rides, that are the preferred nest sites.

Figure 19 Distribution of a "rare event" in a woodland mapped by complete survey

The distribution of wood ant (<u>Formica rufa</u> L.) nests occupied in 1974 in Bedford Purlieus (Cambs) (map produced by R C Welch: reproduced from Peterken & Welch 1975)

Rides are shown by broken lines.

Classification systems

Classification of woodland vegetation in Britain has developed largely independently of continental practice, although Klotzli (1970) provides an account of British woods seen from a European point of view. Tansley (1939) long provided the standard system, but both the woods and classification ideas have changed since the publication of his descriptions. The classification used in A nature conservation review (Ratcliffe 1977; Table 16) is useful for a broad grouping of sites, but is not detailed enough for survey purposes.

Table 16   Classification of woodlands used in A nature conservation review (after Ratcliffe 1977)

Oakwoods	-	western
	-	eastern
Mixed deciduous woodland	-	central facies
	-	lime facies
	-	hornbeam facies
	-	sweet chestnut facies
	-	ancient parks and overmature woodland
Beechwoods		
Ashwoods		
Pinewoods		
Birchwoods		
Alderwoods		
Other types including	-	Holly wood
	-	Yew wood
	-	Juniper wood
	-	Box wood

Classification systems which have been produced in recent years include the "Merlewood" system, which is based on indicator species and primarily uses the ground flora (vascular plants and bryophytes), (Bunce & Shaw 1972, 1973; Bunce 1981, 1982; Rackham 1983) and the work of the Macaulay Institute on the vegetation of Scotland, which follows a continental phytosociological approach with major divisions based largely on the canopy and others on the ground flora (Birse & Robertson 1976; Birse 1980; Robertson 1984). There are also classifications of particular areas, for example of Skye (Birks 1973), the Morrone Birkwoods (Huntley & Birks 1977) and the Scottish native pinewoods (Hill, Bunce & Shaw 1975).

The understorey in ancient woodlands often reflects the history and environmental variations of a site more closely than do the canopy trees, which may have been planted. This has led to the two similar, but independent, systems of Rackham (1980) and Peterken (1980, 1981), the latter probably having the wider application. A different type of canopy classification was developed by Bunce, Munro & Parr (1979) from the results of a survey of Scottish deciduous woodland (Table 2; Figure 4).

An ambitious attempt to apply modern numerical classification ideas and more traditional phytosociology to British woodland forms part of the National Vegetation Classification (NVC), a project funded by the NCC and co-ordinated by Dr J Rodwell at Lancaster University. The project is now in its final phases and the draft woodland chapter has been produced, but it may be a few years before it is fully "road-tested" and operational within the NCC.

Which classification to use?

In all survey work there may be advantages in using more than one system (Frenkel & Harrison 1974), but various factors limit the choice. Birse & Robertson's types are as inappropriate for southern England as Rackham's coppice types are for northern Scotland. Peterken's Stand Type system cannot be used in woods which have been totally converted to plantations. The Merlewood system can only be used effectively if quadrats are recorded. Within any area the range of types from any one of the national systems is usually small, so some subdivisions to fit local circumstances may be essential.

Within my experience the most widely used and useful systems to date have been the Stand Type system and the Merlewood Plot Type classification. Further details of these are given in Appendix 4. These two systems can be usefully combined through a mixture of Stand Type mapping supplemented by selective quadrat recording, with either stratified random or subjective placing of the quadrats in the Stand Type areas (Kirby 1982). The type of combined quadrat record suggested in Appendix 3 does however allow for the use of other systems. The Stand Type system is probably the more generally useful because it depends less on quadrat recording, which is time-consuming, it can be used with free mapping, and it fits more easily with Tansley's types, which are familiar to many ecologists already. (Personal bias on the part of the author is freely admitted here.)

In future the NCC will use the NVC as the main floristic basis for woodland classification, although it will not totally supplant other systems. There are important differences between sites that are better differentiated in other ways, for example the difference between lime-, oak- or hornbeam-dominated variants of the same NVC sub-community. A preliminary description of the NVC woodland classification is given in Appendix 4 with a brief note as to how it may be used in future surveys.

Relationships between types from the different systems

There is a strong trend in British woodland vegetation from south-east to north-west, from low altitudes, often base-rich soils, low rainfall and more continental conditions to high altitudes, more base-poor substrates, high rainfall and Atlantic conditions, and this is reflected in all the major systems. In the circumstances it would be surprising if there was not some association between the types from the different classification systems. A one-to-one relationship should not be expected, however, because of differences in how the systems were derived. The spectrum of variation is split at different points, but samples are placed in roughly the same positions relative to each other by different systems (Table 17). The relationships between types are discussed in more detail by Peterken (1981) and in the NVC woodland chapter.

Table 17   Examples of the relationships between different classification systems

(a)   Classification of quadrat results into both Stand and Plot Types (from Kirby 1984b: reproduced by permission of the Field Studies Council)

The number of quadrats keying out to a particular combination of Plot and Stand Types is shown in each cell of the table.

Mean no. of Plot Types per Stand Type: 5.5 ± 0.4 (n=25)
Mean no. of Stand Types per Plot Type: 6.0 ± 0.8 (n=22)

Mean no. of quadrats per Stand Type: 18.4 ± 4.4 (n=25)
Mean no. of quadrats per Plot Type: 20.9 ± 3.5 (n=22)

Total no. of quadrats recorded: 461

STAND TYPES

(Row-axis label, read vertically down the Plot Type numbers: PLOT TYPES)

Plot Type	7C	10	2A	8E	1C	2B	4C	1A	3A	3C	9A	1D	6D	2C	6C	5B	8A	7E	7Ab	3D	7D	7Aa	6Ac	12	6AB	Total no.
1	2	4	1	1	1	2	1	2																		14
7	3		4	1	1		1	1	3	2	2			7												25
2		1	1								2															4
5	1		1	1	4	1	1	7		1	4	4			1											26
6			4	1	1	1	1	4		1		2		1	1											17
8				2	2								1	1	1											7
12					1			4	1			11	2	5				1	5	19	5					54
P 11							1		2	3		3		1			1	1	5	2					3	22
L 10								5		4		4						13	9	6	1					42
O 13																1			2	1						4
T 30																	1			5	12	2	1	4		25
22													1		1	2	1		1	4		1	7	4		22
23													2		2	2				1			6	3		16
T 24														2		1						1	1			5
Y 15																		1	7	1						9
P 16																			1	9						10
E 26																				1		4	7	3	12	27
S 25																				1			6		41	48
29																				1	4		1	3	13	22
27																				1	4	10	1	3	29	48
18																									9	9
17																									5	5
Total no.	6	5	11	5	10	5	5	23	6	11	8	24	8	19	5	7	5	16	32	51	26	18	30	20	105	461

Table 17   Examples of the relationships between different classification systems

(b)   Classification of quadrats in Scottish birchwoods according to different systems (from Kirby 1984a: reproduced from Transactions of the Botanical Society of Edinburgh by permission of the Editor)

SITE	Torrboll Sutherland	Glen Lonan Argyll	Strathbeg (1) Sutherland	Ardvar Sutherland	Glenralloch Argyll	Dalavich Argyll	Inverpolly (1) Ross	Inverpolly (2) Ross	Strathbeg (2) Sutherland	Geary Ravine Skye
Short Description	*Vaccinium*-rich "heathy" stands		Bryophyte-rich stand	Grass-bracken dominated stands		Wet *Molinia-Sphagnum* stands		Flushed, herb-rich stands		Birch-hazel scrub herb-rich
Peterken (1981) Stand Types	Birch-rowan 12A				Birch-hazel 12B	Birch-rowan 12A	Birch-hazel 12B		Birch-rowan 12A	Birch-hazel 12B
Bunce (1982) Plot Types	*Calluna-Pteridium* type 27				*Succisa-Holcus* type 30	*Narthecium-Molinia* type 28	*Calluna-Pteridium* type 27	*Succisa-Holcus* type 30		
McVean & Ratcliffe (1962)	Betuletum Oxaleto-Vaccinetum				*Betula*-herb nodum			*Fraxinus-Brachypodium sylvaticum* nodum		
Birks (1973)	*Betula pubescens-Vaccinium myrtillus* association						*Betula pubescens-Cirsium heterophyllum* association			*Corylus avellana-Oxalis acetosella* association
Birse & Robertson (1976)	Galio saxatalis – Quercetum association				*Betula pubescens*			No clear equivalent		

Each record consists of a list of vascular plants found within a square quadrat of 200 m² (14.1 x 14.1 m) together with an estimate of the cover within the plot of each species assessed on a Domin scale. Each quadrat has then been assigned to one or other of the "birchwoods" recognised by different systems.

Whole site classifications

Most woods are a mosaic of different vegetation types (however defined). After the development of the Merlewood Plot Type classification a similar type of classification was developed for whole sites based on the data from up to 16 quadrats distributed at random through a wood (R G H Bunce, personal communication). This "Site Type" classification has been used in north and mid Wales (Smith 1981; Day 1986). There are some theoretical objections (Figure 20) to defining a site type on overall composition data without reference to how the species or vegetation types are distributed in the site. Consequently, while there is scope for developing this approach, the existing systems should be used with caution.

Figure 20   Possible limitations to "Site Type" classifications

The Merlewood Site Classification is based on the frequency with which certain species occur in sets of eight or sixteen 200 m^2 quadrats placed randomly in a wood. A problem with this and similar approaches to site type classification is that no account is taken of how the various species or vegetation types in a wood are distributed.

In the example below, woods A and B have the same overall composition and so fall into the same Site Type whereas C, D and E fall into three other Site Types. It would however be as, if not more, logical to compare C, D and E with the appropriate sections of B, but regard the mosaic in A as a completely different type. Although this is a hypothetical example, it is possible to find woods which more or less correspond to A-E in any group of sites.

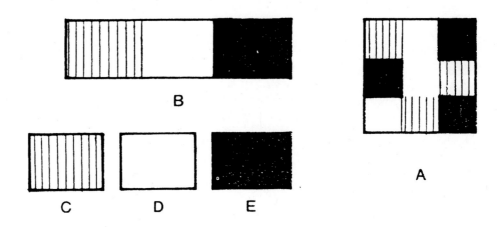

B

C   D   E

A

Sub-site recording

Given that a site can be described and mapped as separate areas, the next logical step is to make separate records for each area. The minimum is a brief description of the main species and structure in note form or using the standard format devised by Jane MacKintosh (Scottish Field Unit) (Table 18). This may be developed as resources permit by recording quadrats within the separate areas and by completing survey forms for the different areas (Figure 21). If this approach is used it is important to try to define the boundaries of the different sub-sites prior to the survey; otherwise different surveyors may use different criteria to define boundaries. In addition, if the surveyor is mapping the sub-sites at the same time as recording them it can be inconvenient to have to keep switching record cards as he/she moves from one sub-site to another.

Table 18 Sub-site records (based on a system used in Scotland devised by Jane MacKintosh)

Stand descriptions follow the following pattern for each separate vegetation or management unit recorded.

Canopy layer (CL)   -   Abundance, height, range and diameter of each species and % cover for the whole layer

Shrub layer (SL)   -   Abundance, height, range and diameter of each species and % cover for the whole layer

Ground flora (GF)   -   A list of the commoner species and their abundance

Any other additional description as appropriate

Example:

CL = Querc. pet. (D), 10-12 m, 15-25 cm; Bet. pub. (O), 7-10 m, 10-15 cm; Sorb. auc. (R), 7m, 5cm. 70%.

SL = Cory. ave. (F), 3-5 m. 30%.

GF = Anth. od. (A), Holc. moll. (A), Gal. sax. (F), Pot. ere. (F), Oxal. acet. (O), Des. flex. (R), Pter. aqu. (LA), Hylo. spl. (O), Rhyt. lor. (O), Pleur. schr. (O), Plag. und. (O), Polyt. form. (O).

Separate records based on compartments as the sub-sites may be needed for management planning, whilst separate records per vegetation type make it easier to judge the importance of a stand as a representative of its type. The larger and more distinct an area is, the more important it is to have a complete separate record. As a rough guide, areas over 30 ha should almost always be subdivided for recording purposes except in the briefest of visits.

Sub-site records can always be combined subsequently, whereas it is not possible to split a composite record down to its sub-site components. However, the practical difficulties of this approach limit the number of surveys where it can be adopted. Where sub-sites are not recorded separately, the notes describing each area become more important and should be made as detailed as possible.

Figure 21 Stages in sub-site recording

(a) The basic record for Dingley Dell identifies three main types (A, C, D) and a fourth type (B) as a narrow strip along a stream (I). The extent and main species for each type are recorded separately, but otherwise the record is a composite one.

(b) As (a) but with separate quadrat records (□) from each type (II).

(c) Four separate records produced, one for each distinct area (A, B, C, D).

(d) As (c) but with quadrat records from each type.

Stages (c) and (d) may present practical difficulties for the surveyor who has no prior knowledge of the variation within the site and takes the route indicated (III). At point Y, the first encounter with type B, it may be considered as just a transition between types A and C and so not worth recording separately. It may only be at Z that it becomes clear that it is a distinct zone that needs separate recording, by which time much of its area (and features) will have been incorporated in the records for A and C.

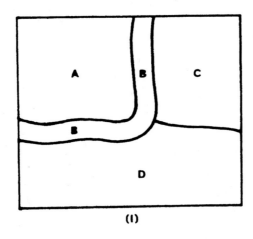

(I)

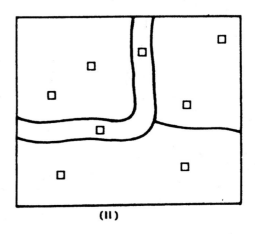

(II)

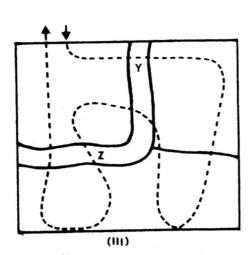

(III)

Woodland structure

Introduction

The following elements of woodland structure may be considered in surveys:

(a) the age distribution of the main canopy species;

(b) the growth form of the trees and shrubs present;

(c) the degree of layering of leaves and branches (vertical structure);

(d) the distribution of different ages, growth forms or layers through the wood (horizontal structure).

Natural structures

Some structural features are of conservation interest in their own right because they approach what might be expected in a natural wood; for instance a canopy gap may be created by a large fallen beech which, if allowed to rot in place, will subsequently fill with self-sown beech seedlings. However, because British woods have been managed intensively in the past, it is debatable what types of structure natural forests would have. Elsewhere in the temperate zone uneven-aged stands may be highly artificial, as in woods managed by selection systems, while even-aged stands may develop after natural catastrophes such as fire or major wind-blow (Jones 1945; Whitehead 1982).

Structure, diversity and management

Elton (1966) drew attention to the importance of woodland structure in the broadest sense as a basis for describing animal habitats. Types of structure that may be particularly valuable for a species or group of species include open rides for butterflies and dense low coppice for nightingales. Structures illustrate the effects of historical events or traditional patterns of management. The structure may also be used as a guide to possible future management: a mature even-aged wood with no regeneration may imply a need for some action to ensure its perpetuation. Where woods are generally open to grazing or browsing animals such as sheep and deer, a common problem in upland areas, assessing the actual or potential regeneration is particularly important.

Assessment of structure

Types of structural analysis that may be considered where resources are available are summarised in Table 19 and Figures 22-24. Structural surveys can often be carried out in winter and indeed may be easier to do then, because the structure is easier to see.

One approach to the estimation of the age distribution of trees in a wood is to use the diameter distribution (conventionally measured at "breast height", 1.3 m) as a substitute for direct age measurements. It must be stressed, however, that there is only a very approximate relationship between the two. Complete enumeration of all the trees in a compartment or wood is used in some forestry systems to provide a check on growth and harvesting rates, but this would not normally be considered in nature conservation surveys. However, a quick picture of the stand structure (Figure 24) can be built up from roughly estimated 10 x 10 m plots within which trees are assigned simply to 10 cm diameter classes.

More detailed structural analysis may involve plotting the positions of the individual trees (Lindsay 1983; Koop 1986; Peterken & Jones 1987).

Although the trees make the most obvious contribution to woodland structure, shrubs and even species such as bramble can be important. Most of the work that has been done to quantify this has been in relation to bird surveys, since foliage density in the 2-4 m height range is well correlated with bird densities. This understorey is also important as competition for ground flora species and as potential food for grazing and browsing mammals. Vertical point quadrats (R Putman pers. comm.), as have been used in peat bogs (Curtis & Bignal 1985), may be one approach worth considering.

Conclusions

Describing woodland structure in detail is beyond the scope of Level 2 surveys. In even the briefest of visits, however, it is possible to identify the main growth forms present and their approximate abundance, to estimate roughly the overall age distribution from the diameters of the trees, to determine the existence and extent of vertical layering, and to indicate through a map or notes whether there is much variation from place to place within the wood. Where quadrats are used, the structure at a given point can be more precisely described, and the results from a set of quadrats can give, for example, a quantitative assessment of mean canopy cover.

Table 19   Woodland structure

Methods of measurement

Measurement of	height	–	hypsometer
	girth/diameter	–	tapes, calipers
	age	–	increment borer,
		–	ring counts on stumps and felled trees
	mean basal area of trees	–	relascope*
	cover	–	estimate subjectively
		–	use a canopy camera with a fish-eye lens (Anderson 1964)
		–	use a periscope device (Emlen 1967)
	foliage density in the understorey	–	estimate subjectively use a siting board

Sampling structure

Transects across selected areas (Peterken & Jones 1987)
Quadrats (see previous section on distribution of quadrats)
Point sampling (Cottam & Curtis 1956; Cameron 1980)
Complete enumerations (Lindley 1976; Archibald 1981)
Photographs of selected areas (NCC 1978)

Some mensurational terms used in forestry

Diameter breast-height (dbh)	–	conventionally measured at 1.3 m above ground
Basal area	–	total area of the tree trunks in cross-section at breast height
Total height	–	height to the top of the tree
Timber height	–	height to the point at which the main stem is less than 7 cm (top diameter) (Smaller stems are considered to have no measurable timber volume.)
Top height	–	the mean total height for the 100 largest-diameter trees per hectare, used in estimating yield class through forestry management tables (Edwards & Christie 1981)
Density	–	number of trees per unit area
Stocking	–	the density of the stand compared to the optimum conventional density for maximum timber production, usually expressed as a percentage

Measurement of timber heights and volumes and other forestry statistics are discussed in Hamilton (1975), James (1982) and Loetsch, Zohrer & Haller (1973).

* This does not provide any indication of whether it is many small trees or one large tree making up the given basal area measurement, but it is a quick and relatively simple procedure. Used in conjunction with some sampling of the size of the trees, it may be worth wider use in nature conservation work.

Figure 22   Recording woodland structure in Level 2 surveys

Age - a seedling, b sapling, c young tree, d mature tree, e over-mature tree

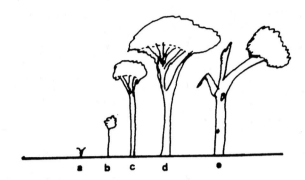

Growth form - a maiden, b coppice stool, c tree singled from coppice, d shrub, e pollard, f climber

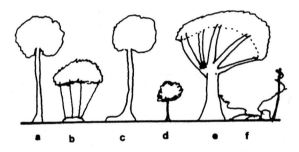

Vertical structure - a field and ground (moss) layer, b shrub (understorey) layer, c tree (main canopy) layer

Horizontal structure - a recently cut hazel coppice, b ride, c 15-yr-old hazel, d ash plantation, e dying elm, f recently cut coppice, g elm, h 25-yr-old Norway spruce

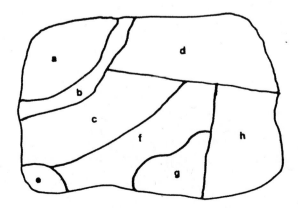

Figure 23 Examples of results from detailed structural surveys

(a) Structure of ash-maple-hazel coppice in Hayley Wood (Cambs). The measured profile is of trees and shrubs over 2 m high in a 4.5 x 24.5 m plot (from Rackham 1975: reproduced by permission from the author and publishers)

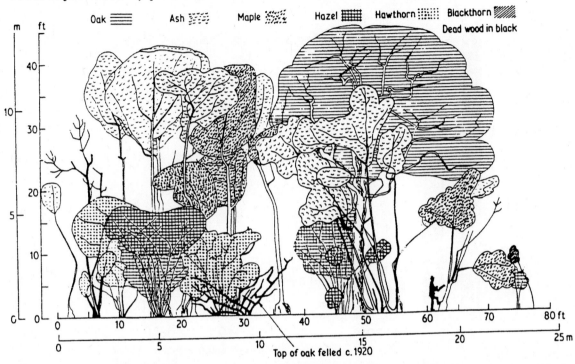

(b) Mapped permanent plots. Each circle shows the location of a stem and is accompanied by a species code (Fr = _Fraxinus_, etc) and the stem diameter (cm) (from measurements in Lady Park Wood (Gloucs) by A Orange; see also Peterken & Jones 1987).

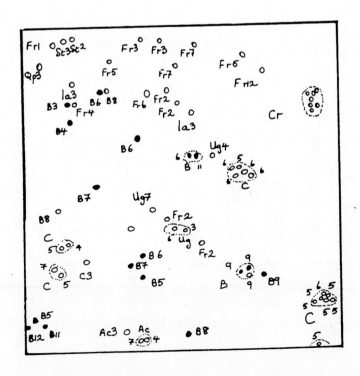

Figure 24 Tree diameter distributions

(a)   The different size (age) structure of ash and oak in a compartment of Bovey
      Woods (Devon) as shown by complete enumeration of the stems (data from Lindley
      1976)

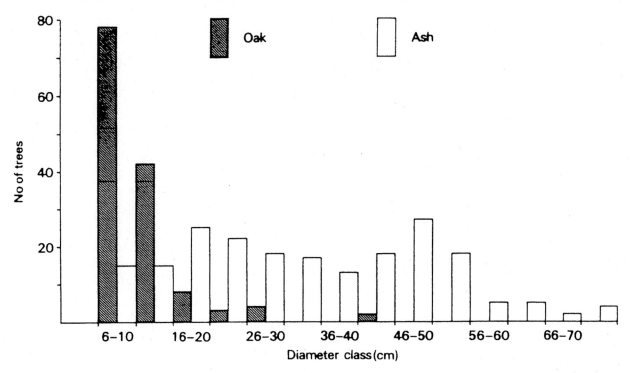

(b)   The growth of neglected ash and sycamore coppice (1974–84) assessed by using
      results from 10 x 10 m quadrats in Wytham Wood (Oxon) (Horsfall & Kirby 1985)

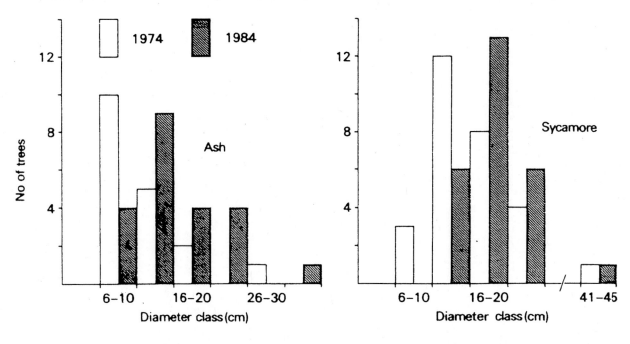

Subsidiary habitats within woodland

Woods may include subsidiary habitats such as glades, rides, ponds, streams and cliffs which add to the nature conservation interest of these sites. Some of these habitats may be large enough to justify detailed survey in their own right; others can be adequately described in a few words.

Various forms have been produced which list different categories of sub-habitat within the woodland, e.g. Table 20. Surveyors then cross off those present in a particular quadrat or wood. This has particular advantages where the results are to be computerised. However, it may not provide as good a picture of the habitat as written notes, as the use of arbitrary categories may attach greater importance to areas than they deserve. It is not clear at what threshold size the importance of, for example, a glade suddenly increases.

Table 20   Part of a recording form for subsidiary habitats within woodland (from Bunce 1982: reproduced by permission of ITE)

C TREES - DEAD (= HABITATS)

35 Fallen brkn.	37 Log. v. rotten	39 Hollow tree	41 Stump <10 cm
36 Fallen uprtd.	38 Fall. bnh. >10 cm	40 Rot hole	42 Stump >10 cm

D TREES - EPIPHYTES AND LIANES

43 Bryo. base	45 Bryo. branch	47 Lichen branch	49 Ivy
44 Bryo. trunk	46 Lichen trunk	48 Fern	50 Macrofungi

E HABITATS - ROCK

51 Stone <5 cm	54 Scree	57 Rock ledges	60 Rock piles
52 Rocks 5-50 cm	55 Rock outcp.<5 m	58 Bryo. covd. rock	61 Exp. grav/sand
53 Boulders >50 cm	56 Cliff >5 m	59 Gully	63 Exp. min. soil

F HABITATS - AQUATIC

63 Sml. pool < $1m^2$	66 Strm/riv. slow	69 Spring	72 Dtch/drain wet
64 Pond 1-20 m^2	67 Strm/riv. fast	70 Marsh/bog	73
65 Pond/lake >20 m^2	68 Aquatic veg.	71 Dtch/drain dry	74

G HABITATS - OPEN

75 Gld. 5-12 m	77 Rky. knoll <12 m	79 Path <5 m	81 Track non-prep
76 Gld. >12 m	78 Rky. knoll >12 m	80 Ride >5 m	82 Track metalled

H HABITATS - HUMAN

83 Wall dry	85 Wall ruined	87 Soil excav.	89 Rubbish dom.
84 Wall mortared	86 Embankment	88 Quarry/mine	90 Rubbish other

Rides have received particular attention in recent years because of their importance for woodland-edge invertebrate communities, especially butterflies (Peachey 1980). Figure 25 illustrates a way in which ride structure may be described with the aim of identifying potentially valuable areas. The cross-section of a ride may be further characterised by recording across it a belt transect subdivided into 1 m sections; variations between different lengths of ride can be assessed by listing the plant species, and especially any good nectar sources, and their abundance in 10-30 m sections. Similarly, surveys specifically for dead wood habitats have been carried out in the New Forest.

Figure 25   Characterisation of rides as habitats for invertebrates by using (a) ride-edge structure (likely value for invertebrates 1<2<3) and (b) the relative abundance of nectar-supplying plant species in different parts of a ride system (≡ high, = medium, - low) (England Field Unit 1982)

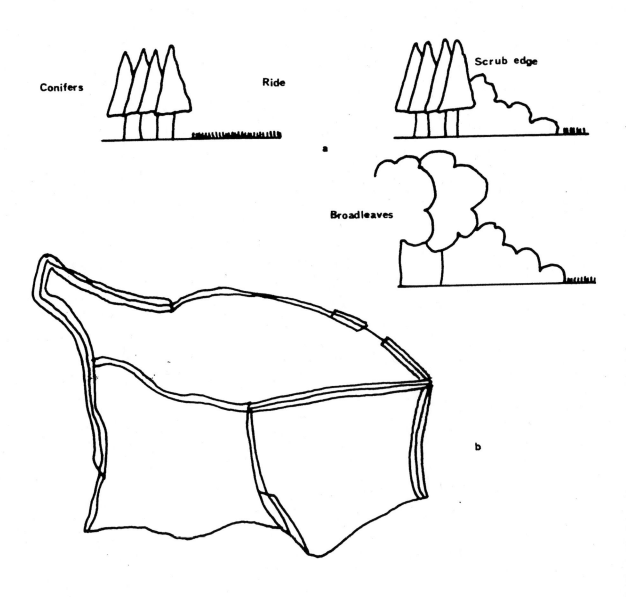

Much information about subsidiary habitats may be shown on annotated site maps. Some of the main features to be looked for and commented on are noted in Table 21.

Table 21   Subsidiary habitats within woodland

Main categories

Openings	clearings and glades, which may be temporary or permanent, plus rides, wayleaves for pylons etc. Factors to consider: size, orientation, nature of transition to woodland, whether temporary or permanent, degree of shading, whether linked to other openings or isolated.
Water bodies	ponds, streams, rivers, springs, fire-ponds, puddles in permanently rutted tracks. Factors to consider: whether moving or still, nature of substrate, depth and type of margin, degree of shading, size, presence of vegetation in or overhanging the water, trophic status.
Rocks	cliffs, gorges, outcrops, screes, surface stone, pavement. Factors to consider: size, type, presence of vegetated ledges (particularly in grazed woodland), bryophyte cover (particularly where there are wet rock faces).
Bogs, fens, flushes	all wet "squidgy" areas, whether on peat or mineral soil. Factors to consider: wetness, presence and depth of peat, acidity, type of vegetation, whether open or shaded.
Dead wood	Factors to consider: abundance and size of logs, whether standing or fallen, in shade or in the open, dead branches or trees, holes in trunks.
Other	old bomb-dumps, gardens, buildings, sawdust heaps, rusting cars.

Species groups other than vascular plants (general)

<u>Introduction</u>

The vascular plant list cannot always be used as a guide to the richness of a wood for other groups of organisms; in western woods, for example, there can be a negative correlation between vascular plant numbers and the abundance of bryophytes (Figure 26). Woods rich in dead wood may have many invertebrates and fungi, but few vascular plants; in the extreme cases of some parklands and heavily grazed woods, the woodland ground flora may have totally disappeared but there may be a rich epiphytic lichen flora and dead-wood beetle fauna associated with the trees (Harding & Rose 1986).

Figure 26   The relationship between the number of vascular plants recorded from a wood and bryophyte cover, estimated from eight randomly placed quadrats for oakwoods in North Wales (from surveys described in Smith 1981; Day 1986)

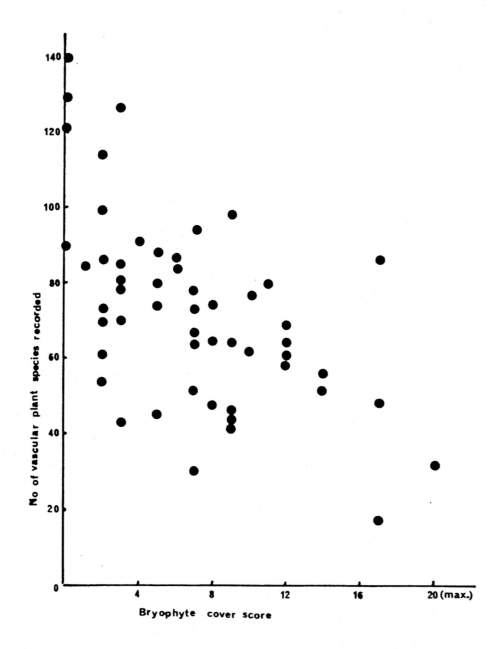

Methods for identifying the other groups of species present in woods are usually more time-consuming than those for vascular plants. They range from relatively unstructured types of survey such as a fungus foray, to systematic, repeated sampling of particular areas as in the Common Bird Census or butterfly transects. Some groups such as bryophytes and lichens may be largely confined to, or most abundant in, particular areas within a wood, so that the non-specialist may find it difficult or impossible to identify likely important sites. The same is true for particular groups of invertebrates.

Local members, conservation committees or national secretaries of organisations such as the British Bryological Society or the British Mycological Society may be able to say which sites they consider to be especially rich or important. With poorly-recorded groups a list of the "best" sites obtained in this way may be little more than an indication of which sites have been regularly visited. It is, however, better than nothing.

The use of lower plants in woodland classification

The National Vegetation Classification and to a lesser extent the Merlewood classification include bryophytes and lichens which may cause problems for some surveyors. Ideally surveyors should try to learn to recognise at least the commoner and more important species in the field (Table 22). A less satisfactory solution is to collect samples which may be identified later. However, there is little point in collecting samples unless there is someone prepared to do the identification. Surveyors should be instructed as to what and what not to collect ("codes of conduct") by whoever will do the identification.

Table 22   Basic bryophyte and lichen list

Mosses

Atrichum undulatum	
Brachythecium rutabulum	B
Ctenidium molluscum	
Dicranella heteromalla	B
Dicranum majus	
D. scoparium	B
Eurhynchium praelongum	B
E. striatum	B
Fissidens taxifolius	B
Hookeria lucens	
Hylocomium splendens	B
H. brevirostre	
Hypnum cupressiforme	B
Isopterygium elegans	B
Isothecium myosuroides	
Leucobryum glaucum	B
Mnium hornum	B
M. undulatum	B
Plagiothecium denticulatum	B
P. undulatum	B
Pleurozium scheberi	B
Polytrichum spp.	B
P. formosum	
P. commune	
Pseudoscleropodium purum	B
Ptilium crista-castrensis	
Rhytidiadelphus loreus	
R. squarrosus	B
R. triquetrus	B
Sphagnum spp.	B
Thamnium alopecurum	B
Thuidium tamariscinum	B

Liverworts

Bazzania trilobata	W
Calypogeia fissa	
Conocephalum conicum	
Diplophyllum albicans	
Herberta adunca	W
Lepidozia reptans	
Lophocolea bidentata	B
L. cuspidata	
Pellia spp.	B
Plagiochila asplenioides	B
P. spinulosa	W
Porella platyphylla	
Scapania gracilis	W
Mylia taylori	W

Lichens

Cetraria glauca	
Cladonia squamosa	
C. coccifera	
C. fimbriata	
Lobaria pulmonaria	
Peltigera canina	
Parmelia caperata	
P. physodes	
P. saxatilis	
Sphaerophorus globosus	
Sticta spp.	
Usnea spp.	

B = used in Bunce's (1982) key
W = western species

Mammals (Dr A Mitchell-Jones)

Introduction

Direct observations of mammals cannot contribute much in Level 2 surveys; more can be gleaned from signs of their presence or activity (Bang & Dahlstrom 1974), and it is possible to draw general conclusions from the habitat structure about whether a site is likely to meet the requirements for a particular species.

Few species of mammal occur only in woodland: most are found in a range of habitats. As most species are not obligate woodland dwellers, it is difficult to assess the overall importance of woodland to mammals; much depends on what alternative habitats are open to them. For example, red deer are really woodland, or woodland edge, animals but they manage to survive on the open hill in Scotland.

Mammals are less dependent on the species composition of a wood than on its structure. Woods with a diverse structure and, more particularly, a thick shrub or herb layer are likely to provide the richest habitats. Patches of scrub can provide shelter and secure lying-up places. Mammals will colonise suitable "new" woodland much more quickly than plants, so that recent semi-natural woodland may support a rich mammal community. To both birds and mammals current productivity and physical structure are more important than long-term habitat continuity.

The particular habitat requirements of different species are noted in Table 23.

The cryptic habits and high mobility of most mammals make them an exceedingly difficult group to survey quantitatively, and it is recommended that quantitative surveys are not even attempted unless there are very good reasons for doing so. If a survey must be done, then indices of abundance are usually more easily obtained than estimates of absolute abundance.

Much of our knowledge of the distribution and relative abundance of species comes from indirect sources such as game bag records or hunting yearbooks (e.g. Game Conservancy Annual Reviews for 1979, 1984; Chanin & Jefferies 1978), from sample surveys that record the presence or absence of a species at a large number of locations (e.g. Lenton, Chanin & Jefferies 1980; Tee, Rowe & Pepper 1985) or from an accumulation of records collected from observers over a period of years (Arnold 1984).

Small mammals

Rats, mice and voles

These species may be most easily surveyed by using baited live-traps (the Longworth trap being the most commonly used for mice and voles) or snap-traps. Establishing the presence of a species is relatively easy and requires only a small number of traps. This may be carried out at any time of year, though the autumn and early winter will be most productive. The establishment of absolute density or even of relative density (e.g. between habitats or between years) is much more time-consuming and involves capture-recapture studies with the traps laid on a grid or transect pattern. Statistical analysis of the results is essential. There is a huge literature on small mammal trapping and capture-recapture methods. Seber (1982) gives a good introduction to the methods and statistical treatment of results, and Gurnell & Flowerdew (1982) deal with the practicalities.

Shrews

Shrews will visit live-traps, presumably out of curiosity, and can also be captured in pitfall traps. Their small size and high metabolic rates mean that they rapidly starve to death if deprived of food and so traps must be inspected frequently. Shrews are on Schedule 5 of the Wildlife and Countryside Act and so a licence is required to trap them.

Table 23   British mammals and their preferred woodland habitats

Species	Woodland type and special requirements
Insectivora	
Hedgehog	Open woods and scrub: ubiquitous.
Mole	All where the soil is deep enough; less common in pure conifer stands.
Common shrew	Open woods with herbaceous layer or grassy clearings.
Pigmy shrew	Open woods with herbaceous layer or grassy clearings.
Water shrew	Open woods with herbaceous layer; may be some distance from water.
Chiroptera	All of these are forest species which require holes or hollow trees in which to roost. Many will use nest-boxes if these are provided in coniferous plantations; research on this continuing.
Brandt's bat	
Bechstein's bat	
Daubenton's bat	
Serotine	
Leisler's bat	
Noctule	
Barbastelle	
Lagomorpha	
Rabbit	All except dense plantations with no herb layer.
Brown hare	Infrequent, but may use woods for shelter.
Mountain hare	Infrequent. Usually on moorland in Scotland and the Peak District. May suffer from afforestation if the amount of moorland is drastically reduced, but this seems unlikely at the moment.
Rodentia	
Red squirrel	Mainly coniferous but also broadleaved. Has suffered a decline in the past 40 years and is now confined to the Breckland forests, North Wales, northern England and Scotland (except central lowlands). Survival in Breckland and Wales in some doubt. Reasons for decline uncertain, but presence of grey squirrel may prevent recolonisation by red squirrel. Particularly associated with Scots pine and requires a selection of mature stands of different ages. However, the planting of "amenity belts" may allow the grey squirrel to move in.
Grey squirrel	Broadleaved and sometimes coniferous. A major pest in places and can cause considerable damage, especially to hardwood plantings. Likely to extend its range at the expense of the red squirrel.

Bank vole	All with dense ground cover.
Field vole	All with grass layer. Young plantations can provide an ideal habitat.
Wood mouse	Woods with open field layer. Probably the most common rodent in mature plantations.
Yellow-necked mouse	Similar to wood mouse, but distribution restricted to south-east England and possibly east Midlands.
Brown rat	All woods, especially in summer. Most common near buildings.
Dormouse	Woods with dense shrub layer and nut-bearing trees. Particularly associated with hazel (coppice). A species of restricted distribution which is likely to suffer particularly from habitat destruction and the replacement of semi-natural woodland by conifers. "Traditional" management for coppice is beneficial.
Edible dormouse	Broadleaved woodland; restricted to the Chilterns.

Carnivora

Fox	Ubiquitous. Probably highest density in semi-natural woodland with good populations of small mammals.
Pine marten	Coniferous and broadleaved. Suffered from persecution in 19th century, but thought to be extending its range. Has probably benefited from afforestation. Mainly in Scotland.
Stoat	All woodland with rabbits and small mammals.
Weasel	All woodland with small mammals. Young plantations favoured.
Polecat	All lowland woodland in Wales. Spreading to England. Has probably benefited from afforestation.
Badger	Mainly broadleaved but also in plantations where soil is suitable for setts.
Wild cat	All woodland in the Scottish Highlands. Probably spreading and likely to have benefited from afforestation.

Artiodactyla

Muntjac	Scrub and woodland with dense understorey.
Fallow deer	Open broadleaved with scrub patches for shelter.
Sika deer	Broadleaved and lowland coniferous.
Red deer	Broadleaved and coniferous. A woodland-edge animal.
Chinese water deer	Scrub and woodland with dense shrub layer.
Roe deer	Open woods with scrub; young plantations. This species has extended its range greatly in recent years, probably because of afforestation.

Medium-sized insectivores, rodents and lagomorphs

Insectivores

There is virtually no published methodology for quantitative surveys of either moles or hedgehogs, though presence or absence can be established without much difficulty.

Medium-sized rodents

The presence or absence of red and grey squirrels can easily be established visually but density estimation is difficult. Live-trapping is possible, using cage traps, and densities have been estimated using capture-recapture methods. Drey counts are possible but are not directly related to the number of squirrels, as individuals may construct a number of dreys and may also use hollow trees. Gurnell (1983) provides a review of the subject and Don (1985) discusses the use of drey counts.

Lagomorphs

Lagomorphs are not usually associated with woodland and the survey methodologies that have been developed have all concentrated on quantifying the density of these species on agricultural land (or moorland for the mountain hare) (Barnes & Tapper 1985). The MAFF have developed methods of assessing rabbit density by counts at dusk along hedgerows and field edges, but these methods are not appropriate for woodland.

Bats

Even establishing the presence or absence of particular species can be a problem because of the difficulties of field identification. Putting up bat boxes may help by making the bats easier to find and identify, but there is no established relationship between the number of bats found in bat boxes and the density of bats in an area. Mist-netting can also help with identification, but it is doubtful whether the information gained is worth the risk of physical injury to the bats. Quantitative surveys of bat density are still in their infancy but some progress in comparing densities between areas has been made by using bat detectors either at fixed points or on walked or driven transects. Little of this work has yet been published (Ahlen 1981).

Carnivores

All carnivores are difficult to survey at anything other than a qualitative level and, in general, it is best to work on indices of abundance from signs rather than trying to estimate absolute abundance.

Stoats and weasels

These smaller species can be live-trapped with a fair degree of success, so mark and recapture methods are possible though time-consuming (King 1975). Signs are less obvious than with the larger mustelids and have not been used as indices of abundance.

Mink, pine marten and polecat

Both live-trapping and surveying by signs have been used for these medium-sized mustelids (Velander 1983). Live-trapping is very labour-intensive and a large area must be covered because of the relatively large home ranges of these animals. Mink are perhaps the easiest of the three to catch, as much of their activity is centred on river banks or coasts (Dunstone & Birks 1983). Surveys for droppings (scats) have been more widely used and give a relative index of abundance in different habitats or in different years.

Badger

Badgers live in social groups of varying size with activity centred around a sett. Locating the setts and establishing whether they are occupied or not is a relatively straightforward operation, leaving only the difficulty of estimating the size of the social group. This is best done by counting at dusk as the badgers emerge. The size of the group's home range has been calculated by feeding the badgers with bait containing coloured markers and then searching the dung pits to pinpoint the edge of the group's territory (Kruuk & Parish 1982). Radio-tracking has also been used. See Neal (1986) for a review of methodologies.

Fox

The fox is not confined to woodland but will use woodland as part of a home range. Presence can almost be assumed but can be checked from sightings or droppings. Quantitative surveys have relied mainly on live-trapping and radio-tracking to establish group sizes and home ranges (Lloyd 1980).

Otter

Recent radio-tracking studies show that otters can spend a surprising amount of time (52%) in woodland, though signs are difficult to find. The most productive qualitative survey method is to examine river banks etc for droppings (spraints), which are quite distinctive (Lenton, Chanin & Jefferies 1980).

Wild cat

No quantitative surveys for wild cat have been carried out, but presence or absence can be determined by sightings, perhaps by local people.

Deer

Although a qualitative survey for deer presents no real problems, quantitative surveys in woodland have proved extremely difficult, despite a considerable amount of work on the subject. Indices of abundance have proved more useful and a number of studies have examined the use of dung counts for estimating numbers (e.g. Neff 1968; Mitchell & Cowan 1983).

Grazing surveys

Grazing and browsing by sheep and deer are a major problem in woods (mainly upland), not least because it is difficult to assess how much use is being made of the woods and relate this to observed levels of damage to the regeneration or to changes in the ground flora. An index of deer use in pinewoods based on dung counts is given in Sykes, Marrs & Mitchell (1985), while Putman (1986) describes a series of surveys related to grazing by cattle and ponies in the New Forest. Ways of measuring the effects of sheep-grazing in woodland are being investigated by Dr F Mitchell (Macaulay Land Use Research Institute, Penicuik).

Invertebrates (Dr I F G McLean, A E Stubbs and P Wormell)

Introduction

Information on how to carry out invertebrate sampling and surveys is contained in Stubbs (1979) and Southwood (1978). Dr D Sheppard (NCC, England Field Unit) is currently preparing a review of invertebrate survey methods for NCC staff. Various major surveys have been carried out through the Commissioned Research Programme, e.g. surveys of mature timber habitat (Harding 1978) and the work of the Invertebrate Site Register project. A technique has also been developed for monitoring butterflies on a regular basis (Pollard 1977; Pollard, Hall & Bibby 1986).

During Level 2 surveys it may be possible to note any butterflies seen (Thomas 1983) if the weather is right, but otherwise it is necessary to rely on habitat features as a guide to likely invertebrate diversity on a site.

General points

Woodland is the richest of all invertebrate habitats and mixed deciduous woodlands composed of indigenous species support the most diverse invertebrate communities. Not only do the trees themselves provide food for hundreds of species of insects, but the physical conditions and microclimates found in woods (diffuse light, deep shade, shelter and protection from frost) and the abundance of dead wood, macrofungi and plant litter provide suitable conditions for rich invertebrate populations.

The structural diversity of woodland has enabled invertebrates to exploit a great range of niches; plants have been less successful in accomplishing this feat as epiphytes in the temperate zone. Plantations of exotic trees are relatively poor invertebrate habitats. Uniform stands of native trees are poorer than more diversely structured woods.

The most important woods in terms of entomological interest are those composite sites containing a wide range of native trees and shrubs (including alder and sallow carr) with open flowery glades, patches of peatland, marsh and fen, streams and pools, and dry sunny knolls.

Dead or dying trees, prostrate or upright, and the presence of dead braches on living trees provide breeding grounds for bark- and wood-boring beetles, wood wasps and their parasites. Decaying trees and fungi support a wealth of beetles, particularly Staphylinidae, and fungivorous flies of the Mycetophilidae, Helonyzidae, Clusiidae and Clythiidae as well as their muscid predators.

Suntraps in flowery woodland glades, particularly in woods with a southerly aspect, provide conditions for rich insect populations. Butterflies such as the pearl-bordered fritillary and chequered skipper rely on these conditions.

An open area of peatland in an exposed situation usually supports a rather restricted range of insects, but small areas of valley peatland surrounded by wooded slopes, a formation often encountered in the western oceanic oakwoods of Argyll, are rich in invertebrates, particularly where they are fringed with sallow carr.

Woodland site factors

Floral species diversity - trees, shrubs and ground flora

The following trees are important as host species to a wide range of insects; they are listed approximately in order of importance: oak, sallows (Salix spp.), aspen, birch, hawthorn, hazel, alder, lime, wych elm, ash, rowan, gean, sloe, bird cherry, Rosa spp. Some insects, particularly moths, are not restricted to any single tree species and will subsist on introduced trees and shrubs as well as the full range of native species. There are a few which are restricted to certain non-native trees. Some native trees, e.g. holly, do not support a rich invertebrate fauna, but the species they do support may not subsist on anything else. Scots pine and juniper support their own characteristic invertebrate populations, but some insects usually associated with Scots pine will subsist on other Pinus spp.

The epiphyte flora may also be exploited by invertebrates, but relatively few are specific. The larvae of a number of moths of the family Geometridae, e.g. the dotted carpet, feed on epiphitic lichens, preferring Usnea spp., but do not seem to be confined to a particular species. The presence of epiphytic ferns and a structural variety of mosses and lichens is more likely to be significant than diversity of species. Similarly, the best sites for fungus fauna are not necessarily those with the greatest fungal species diversity.

Woodland structure

Many species are confined to particular structural settings rather than plant species and they may have different needs at different parts of their life cycle.   Various phytophagous species have niche separation even on the same tree or herb, in respect of height above ground or degree of shade. Thus a varied structure is desirable. A thick litter layer is important to many species, although a variety of ground conditions through to bare ground is most valuable. Open structured woods are preferable to those with a dense canopy. Coppice woodland is a special class of open structured woodland.

Edge quality

The best rides and glades are those that receive plenty of sun and contain a diverse flora with a good representation of flowers attractive to insects through the seasons. Shrub edges can be important. The same considerations apply to wood margins. A wood margin hard against intensively farmed land is less likely to be of interest than a wood abutting a meadow (old drove track, wide verge grassland, marshland etc) with plenty of flowers.

Quality of dead wood

Emphasis is placed upon dead wood in the form of large mature trees, whether dead or live with large dead portions. Even in woods without dead trees, the presence of live trees with hollow trunks can be important; entrance to hollows is often present in the fork between root bases (Stubbs 1972).

Old trees

There is good reason to believe that old live trees support a special invertebrate fauna, the most obvious point being that deep crevices in bark are required by some species.

Continuity

Primary or ancient woodland is more likely to support a rich fauna, especially in terms of the soil and litter fauna (Boycott 1934; Hammond 1974; Hunter 1977). Continuity of open ground is particularly important, whether it is as rides and glades or recently cut coppice. Once a woodland canopy has closed up, a significant element of the fauna is lost; when the canopy is reopened the wood may look marvellous, but the fauna is likely to be impoverished for some time.

Shelter

Woods in topographically sheltered positions or on slopes with a southerly aspect are likely to be of greatest interest. However, a large wood can provide shelter within it and compensate for topographic exposure to some degree. A ride system may funnel wind through a wood, a problem which does not arise if rides have bends or T junctions. The exposure factor is of greatest consequence in upland situations and in areas near the coast subject to cold winds in the spring.

Soil conditions

A dry well-drained wood has much less scope for diversity than one with moist or locally wet soils, and the best situations have both moist and dry soil types present. Seepage woodland (usually a form of carr) is a particularly important invertebrate habitat.

Whilst a base-rich woodland soil is possibly able to support the richest invertebrate life, there is no strong evidence to suggest that soil type need be an issue in site selection since each type is likely to have its special features. Groups such as snails prefer calcareous soils, but equally other groups have species which thrive on acid soils. A variety of soil types in a wood will contribute to the variety of invertebrates.

Presence of springs, streams and ponds

Springs within woodland may be very important in some parts of the country. In the Weald, for instance, there are relict northern "glacial" species in cold springs. Streams and rivers within a wood, or along the edge, add considerably to the invertebrate value.

Densely shaded ponds can support a small but characteristic fauna, but on the whole an open sunny pond in a glade, perhaps with local carr margins, is far better. Ponds situated on wood margins, especially those with a sunny aspect, may be equally advantageous. The main point to look for is the presence of shallow or gently-sloping margins with a good vegetation structure (e.g. rushes or sedges); sharp-edged clay pits and gravel pits in woods tend to be poor. Interesting invertebrate populations, including some rare aquatic beetles, are associated with red deer wallows in some Scottish woods.

Presence of "good" insect flowers

A seasonal succession of suitable flowers is required. When little else is in flower, sallows attract many moths, particularly Orthosia spp. in the early spring, whilst ivy flowers are a favourite source of food for insects flying in the late autumn. Good shrubs and trees include sallow, sloe, hawthorn, lime and ivy. Good herbs include bluebell, bugle and foxglove, but especially umbellifers and composites.

Presence of sunny banks (including those on woodland edges)

Eroded banks at the edge of forest rides or in old quarries and pits, where the substrate is dry clay sand and the aspect sunny for several hours during the heat of the day, provide conditions favourable for the burrows of solitary bees and wasps. Such conditions readily become overgrown and shaded, so may only retain their interest if management is favourable.

Grazing

A wood which is intensively grazed has a poor ground flora, and shrubs and seedling trees are usually heavily browsed. Invertebrate populations which subsist on herbs, woodland grasses and shrubs are impoverished both under the trees and in glades and rides. However, no grazing at all may, in some places, result in a reduction of herbs, particularly in open areas, and the excessive growth of certain grasses, while favouring grass-feeding species, may reduce the overall invertebrate diversity.

Grazing by sheep alone often results in a spread of bracken, favouring the limited range of invertebrates which subsist on bracken. Cattle tend to reduce the spread of bracken and encourage the herb component and associated invertebrates, provided that grazing intensity is kept to a low level. Cow dung is by far the richest dung for Muscid flies. Seasonal light grazing by red or fallow deer and the presence of roe usually contribute to the invertebrate fauna. Provided that grazing levels can be maintained at a low enough intensity to allow some natural regeneration and maintain rich assemblages of tall herbs, grasses and ferns, grazing animals can enrich insect populations considerably. The combination of woodland shelter and large mammals provides ideal conditions for a wide range of parasites and bloodsucking Diptera, as well as dung flies and beetles.

Burning

In Scotland many woods suffer annually from fires associated with the sheep-grazing regime. This does not improve the grazing potential in woods and is detrimental to invertebrate populations. Woods which are burnt through regularly are usually poor in all invertebrates except those associated with the upper layers.

Scrub relics and isolated trees

Even remote Hebridean islands which have been almost denuded of their original scrub woodland can support a surprisingly diverse woodland insect fauna. On Rhum National Nature Reserve, which until the end of the last century had been without woodland for two hundred years, over 130 species of moths have been recorded whose larvae feed on trees and bushes in restored woodlands. Of the 72 species of craneflies recorded on the island, over 20 are woodland species, most of these breeding in leaf mould or moist woodland soils and the larvae of a few being found in rotten wood or woodland fungi. Arboreal insects can survive in even the smallest fragments of relict woodland. On the island of Colonsay a thriving colony of purple hairstreak butterflies has survived in a small wind-shaped oak wood where the trees are no more than 5 m high. In open glades in this wood ringlet butterflies are also abundant. These two species are rare on the adjacent mainland of Argyll. Isolated trees have been found in remote glens in the Hebrides which support populations of tree-feeding caterpillars of moths, the females of which are flightless. Some other woodland species whose larvae usually feed on the leaves of trees and shrubs have adapted to feeding on heather, e.g. the dotted border and magpie moths. Invertebrate surveys should therefore not exclude isolated scrub relics in remote situations.

Birds (Dr R J Fuller, British Trust for Ornithology)

Introduction

The following notes provide some general comments on the habitat features of woodland likely to be particularly significant in determining the type of bird community found. Fuller (1982), Fuller & Taylor (1983), Massey (1974) and Williamson (1964, 1970, 1976) indicate the species likely to be found in different woodland types. Some recommendations on methods of counting breeding birds in woodlands are also given, but for detailed appraisals of particular methods consult the literature cited and/or contact the Populations Research Section of the British Trust for Ornithology (BTO) at Beech Grove, Tring, Hertfordshire HP23 5NR.

Broadleaved woodland supports more species of breeding birds than any other habitat in Britain (Fuller 1982). The densities of birds breeding in woodland can also be higher than in any other terrestrial habitat, but there is much variation between individual woods. Many bird species common in woodland are widespread in other habitats such as farmland and gardens, e.g. wren, robin, blue tit, great tit and chaffinch. There are, however, several species which are more or less confined to woodland and/or scrub. These species include the woodpeckers, tree pipit, nightingale, redstart, garden warbler, blackcap, wood warbler, chiffchaff, pied flycatcher, marsh tit, willow tit, nuthatch, treecreeper and hawfinch.

Birds depend more on the structure of the woodland than on the tree species composition. Some species show fairly broad habitat requirements, occurring in many different types of woodland, but several depend on particular habitat features such as early successional stages or scrub. The history of the wood is generally of less significance to birds than to other groups such as plants and insects. This is probably because birds are extremely mobile and can colonise suitable habitats with relative ease. The recent management is a primary factor influencing the birdlife of a wood. The relative abundance of different bird species can change very quickly after alterations to the woodland as a result of management.

Habitat features

Some of the more important features of broadleaved woodland from an ornithological viewpoint are considered below. Relationships between woodland structure and the parameters of bird communities are often complex, and the causal mechanisms behind such relationships are frequently not understood.

Shrub layer

Many species of birds forage and/or nest in the shrub layer. In general, the greater the development of foliage in approximately the lower 4 to 5 m, the richer the bird community in terms of numbers of species and densities of birds. Several warblers, for example blackcap and garden warbler, strongly prefer woodland with a well-developed shrub layer; heavily grazed woods are generally poor for these species.

Woodland edges

The density of several species of songbirds is often greater at the edge of a wood, especially in the outer 50 m, than in the interior. This is usually because the shrub layer is better developed at the edge of woods. Warbler territories are often located at the edges of glades and rides when there is a good development of shrubs. Rides with sharp edges and little shrub growth are not particularly attractive to birds.

Mature trees

Several species are more abundant in woods dominated by mature trees than in woods with few mature trees. Nuthatches are confined to mature woodland, and densities of other hole-nesting birds such as woodpeckers and tits are also greatest in such habitats.

Scrub and coppice

Several long-distance migrants such as tree pipit, nightingale and warblers prefer early successional stages. Tree pipit, for example, often rapidly colonises freshly cut coppice but soon declines as the coppice starts to grow. Nightingales prefer dense thicket scrub or young coppice with a particularly vigorous field layer. In coppice systems many species are quickly lost as the canopy closes over, after which time the typical species are thrushes and tits. Over-mature or neglected coppice is generally a poor habitat for birds.

Methods of counting birds

Many techniques have been used to count birds in woodland: the literature is huge and potentially daunting (see, for example, Ralph & Scott 1981). There is no single "best method". The choice of method should be influenced by the aim of the work being undertaken. Several general points should be borne in mind concerning methods of counting birds. The first is that few methods provide absolutely accurate estimates of densities of birds. Counts should generally be treated as relative estimates, or indices, of abundance. Secondly, it is generally easier to make comparisons of abundance within species than between species. This is because each bird species varies in conspicuousness. Comparisons between species of numbers of birds seen and/or heard will rarely reflect their true relative abundances, unless some species-specific corrections are made to allow for conspicuousness. Many other factors can affect the efficiency of counts, including the weather, the time of day, the time of the year and the ability of the observer (see papers in Ralph & Scott 1981 for further details). In general, one should aim to conduct counts in different study sites in such a way that potential biases from such sources are kept as constant as possible between sites.

In recent years two methods have been particularly favoured by ornithologists in Britain for counting woodland birds. One is a point count method, the other a territory mapping method. Although widely used in Scandinavian forests, line transects have recently found little favour in British woodlands, perhaps because transect techniques are best suited to extensive areas of reasonably uniform habitat.

Point counts

Point count methods are well-suited to surveys where the aim is to make comparisons of the relative abundance of bird species in a series of woods or study areas. There are many variants of point counts, but they all have one feature in common: an observer remains at one location (station) for a predetermined period of time during which he/she records the numbers of birds detected. Each count made in this way is treated as one sample and several such samples are taken within each study area.

A point count method developed by Colin Bibby of the Royal Society for the Protection of Birds, which has been used successfully in several different types of British woodlands, is described below. Examples of the use of this method include a study of western oakwood bird communities by Bibby & Robins (1985) and one of upland conifer plantations by Bibby, Phillips & Seddon (1985).

A series of randomly selected stations are chosen in each study area. (Bibby & Robins chose 10 stations in each wood.) Stations should be positioned at least 100 m apart to reduce the chance of counting the same birds at different stations. In the case of very heterogeneous woods, stratified random sampling may be necessary to ensure that each stand type is sampled appropriately. At each station the observer records birds for five minutes. Counts of birds made within 25 m of the observer ("near" records) are kept separate from those beyond ("far" records). Two visits are made to each station - one in mid April to early May, the other in mid May to early June. For each species, the total number of birds counted is calculated separately for each visit. The higher of the two totals is then used as an index of abundance for the species. Where comparisons of abundance between species are not required, the full data (i.e the sum of near and far records) can be used. Techniques are available for making use of the ratio of near to far records to enable comparisons between species. Point counts can be used to provide much information on the habitat requirements of birds, particularly when measurements of vegetation structure are made at each of the recording stations.

Territory mapping

Territory mapping is far more labour-intensive than point counts and is appropriate for the detailed study of particular sites. For example, territory mapping can be extremely useful in studying the detailed distribution of birds in relation to habitat features within a given wood. It is also appropriate for the long-term study of bird communities in relation to habitat management at selected sites. A strong feature of the method is that it can give a picture of the spatial distribution of birds throughout the study area, unlike point counts, which provide discontinuous information. Territory mapping is the best method to use if a complete census of all birds is required (Tomialojc 1980; O'Connor & Fuller 1984). The method is used by the British Trust for Ornithology in its Common Bird Census project, which monitors annual population levels of breeding birds on selected farmland and woodland study plots (Marchant 1983). Full details of the method are not given here, but are available on request from the BTO.

Territory mapping establishes the numbers and distributions of birds by combining information from a large number of visits. The observer makes 10 visits to the study area between early April and early July. On each visit the positions and activities of all birds seen and/or heard are plotted on 1:2500 maps. Particular attention is paid to recording simultaneous registrations of singing birds. For each species, the pattern of registrations is subsequently interpreted, according to clearly defined rules, in terms of numbers of territories. To obtain the best results from territory mapping it is important to cover the plot very thoroughly on each visit. Each visit should be carried out slowly (in broadleaved woodland it usually takes 1.5 to 2 hours to cover 10 hectares), and the entire study plot should be covered evenly, by ensuring that the observer gets to within at least 50 m of every part of the study area. To be sure of locating one's position when conducting a woodland territory mapping census, it is usually necessary to establish a grid of markers throughout the study area.

Figure 27   Example of bird territory mapping results (data suplied by the British Trust
for Ornithology)

Part of a completed visit map for a woodland census, reproduced at the 1:2500 scale as
used in the field.   It was a productive visit and all parts of the map are crowded with
registrations.   The dotted lines will be particularly helpful in the later analysis of
territories.   Blackbird registrations have already been copied to the species map and
cancelled with a light stroke of the pen.

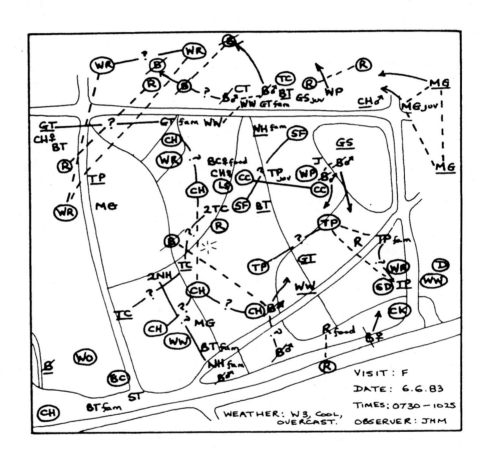

Epiphytes, particularly lichens (R G Woods)

Introduction

The trunks and branches of trees and shrubs (phorophytes) provide a substrate for the growth of many other plants. Rose (1974) lists 65 species of bryophytes and over 300 species of lichens (22% of the British lichen flora) as being recorded from oak in Britain. Many of these species occur on no other substrate. In many woodlands epiphytes account for over half the total plant species diversity of a site.

Rose (1974, 1976) recognised a number of epiphytes as being characteristic of woods of ancient origin which have probably been little disturbed. It is suspected that many of these species are either poor colonisers of newly created habitats or specifically require niches only found on trees of great age. They may prove to be useful indicators of sites likely to support other groups requiring similar conditions, e.g. wood-boring insects.

The British epiphytic lichen flora is internationally important. Surveys of the Low Countries, northern France except Brittany, most of Germany and Denmark have failed to reveal any sites approaching in diversity the best 40 in the British Isles. Whole communities recognised as widespread in this country are only represented elsewhere in North-West Europe as fragments. Some epiphytic habitats are probably among the most threatened in this country. Gilbert (1977) lists the reasons for conserving lichen-rich habitats, as follows.

(a)   Lichens cannot at present be permanently cultured; they have to be safeguarded under natural conditions.

(b)   For its size Britain has a very varied lichen flora including a strong Atlantic element, of which more fragments survive here than in other industrialised parts of North and West Europe.

(c)   Lichen-rich sites frequently show a high degree of correlation with areas of general ecological interest, though not necessarily with a rich higher plant flora.

(d)   A considerable number of fungal and animal species depend on lichens for their survival.

Many of these reasons also apply to bryophytes. Epiphytes are threatened by destruction of woodland, felling of trees, planting of unsuitable host trees, unsuitable forest management such as coppicing, toxic levels of atmospheric sulphur dioxide and other chemicals produced by industry, drift of artificial fertilisers from farmland, and the drying-out of phorophytes by land drainage, which reduces general atmospheric humidity.

There are few sites unaffected by at least one of the above factors. The epiphyte-rich sites which do survive have rarity value if nothing else and should be carefully recorded and conserved.

Initial surveys

Whilst ideally the epiphytic species present in each wood should be recorded, it is recognised that, as the majority are lower plants, their identification is frequently considered to be possible only by a specialist. In fact they need present no greater challenge than the higher plants, with probably a similar proportion of common species being easily identified in the field. However, the following criteria, if met in whole or in part by a site, would suggest that the site is suitable for further study as it may have a rich epiphyte flora.

Low levels of atmospheric sulphur dioxide (less than 50 g m^{-3} mean winter level)

In areas with higher sulphur dioxide levels, sites sheltered in valleys, especially if the valley runs at an angle to the prevailing wind, may still be species-rich. Elm, ash, elder and field maple all have a relatively nutrient-rich bark and their epiphytes resist the effects of sulphur dioxide better than those on the more acidic bark of oak, alder and birch. However, a great range of response appears to be possible within one species and occasionally, for example, an oak may support a community of high-nutrient-demanding species, whilst those around, of similar age and size, appear to be much more acidic. Note the presence of any trees which appear to differ in their epiphytes from the rest.

Large or old trees present, especially if their trunks are well lit

Old trees provide a range of niches not found on immature trees, such as dry bark recessess and dead standing decorticate (bark-free) wood, and are therefore more species-rich. Bark, as it ages, tends to become less acid and consequently supports a different flora from that on younger trees. Old trees consequently support a characteristic climax epiphytic vegetation which is now extremely rare. A policy of removal of old trees is pursued with vigour in most existing, heavily managed, woodlands. The large stools of coppiced trees and pollarded stems can at times support a notable flora, generally richer in bryophytes than lichens, since the latter are less able to tolerate the fluctuating light and humidity of coppiced or pollarded woodland. Similarly, standard trees in coppice-with-standards, whilst usually of more interest than the coppice stems, support fewer species than might be expected. In areas of low sulphur dioxide levels large trees around the woodland edge may be much richer in species than those within a dense wood, whilst the reverse may be true in areas with higher sulphur dioxide levels.

High humidity in the wood

It is notable that the richest epiphyte floras are encountered in areas of high humidity such as woodlands on the west coast affected regularly by sea mist. However, very high rainfall causes leaching and acidification of tree bark and produces characteristic, though less species-rich, communities. In the lowlands, drainage of land has reduced humidity levels. Ill-drained woods in hollows may therefore be expected to be more species-rich and support a more natural flora than those on drained exposed sites.

Sites with a recorded history of continuous cover of mature timber

Rose (1976) deals in detail with this subject, demonstrating that many of the richest sites for lichens have a long history of non-silvicultural management, for example the New Forest, where mature and over-mature timber has been present for hundreds of years. It is important to note that many fine epiphyte sites would be considered to be very poor woodlands, for example medieval deer parks grazed for centuries with only small groups of trees remaining. Only a few very old oaks would be required to support a very respectable epiphyte flora. Crag woodlands in the west and north, which produce timber that is so bent or inaccessible that it is never harvested, are also important.

Sites displaying one or more of the above features may well support a rich epiphyte flora. The next step is to prepare a species list.

Random sampling of epiphytic vegetation to produce a reasonably complete species list is impracticable owing to the abundance of niches, which must all be sampled separately. With experience, adequate lists can be speedily produced by examining the range of phorophyte species present and selecting specimens of varying age in various topographical positions. The Biological Record Centre's record cards for lichens and bryophytes are available.

This is a task for any time of the year, though it is probably marginally better carried out when the trees are free of leaves and the light conditions are better, making species identification easier.

Recording communities

Communities can be described and evaluated with the aid of the works of Barkman (1958) and James, Hawksworth & Rose (1977). The following technique, based largely on Braun-Blanquet methodology, is suggested as the most cost-effective approach.

A site should be extensively searched and the range of niches available on all species of phorophyte examined. Notes taken of the commonest combinations of species will aid in the detection of future relevé sites. All preconceived ideas as to likely associations should be set aside during this phase, the objective being to select sample points which will describe the vegetation of the study site. The subjective selection of sample sites is justified in view of the extreme difficulty of adequate random selection of sample points to describe the total range of vegetation. Many communities are so limited in their requirements, e.g. dry bark recesses, that random sampling of trees to ensure the description of such areas takes an unacceptably long time.

Table 24   Information included on an epiphytic community recording sheet

Site name

Grid reference   Recorder   Date

Sample no.
Tree species
Trunk circumference (cm)
Inclination (degrees)
Aspect
Sample height (cm)
Sample area (cm)
% cover
No. of species
List of species recorded

Once a uniform stand of vegetation has been identified, details of the stand and species present should be recorded (Table 24). The height of the relevé is measured from the ground vertically to the centre of the relevé. The trunk circumference is also measured at the centre of the relevé. Relevé size is typically the largest conveniently-sized area of uniform vegetation up to about 0.5 m². The shape of the relevé will also vary to fit the community. The inclination is recorded in degrees as the angle made between an imaginary horizontal line and a line drawn down the centre of the relevé from top to bottom. Thus angles between 1° and 89° indicate a tree leaning towards an observer on the relevé side, an angle of 90° a vertical tree, and an angle between 91° and 179° a tree leaning away from the observer on the relevé side. The aspect is that of the centre of the relevé recorded as a cardinal point of the compass.

About five relevés are required from each uniform stand in order to determine its phytosociological position. Such relevés need not be taken from the same tree, and indeed Barkman records releves produced by amalgamating data from several branches of one or more trees; for example more than one elder tree may have to be included in a relevé adequately to describe the species-rich Cryphaeetum arboreae. For details concerning the construction of floristic tables, see Chapter 6 of Shimwell (1971). Once discrete noda have been established, James, Hawksworth & Rose (1977) and Barkman (1958) should be consulted to assign noda to recognised associations or alliances. Community data can be used in much the same way as species data in providing an assessment of a site. Unfortunately so little phytosociological data has been published that countrywide comparisons are possible only at the most general level.

Site evaluation

Straight comparisons of diversity are possible. Generally, the larger the species list, the better the site. Any unnatural disturbance is likely to reduce the number of species present, though exceptions occur, such as limestone dust pollution, which in small quantities will increase diversity, and light grazing, which might lead to the development of open areas, also favouring species diversity.

Whilst a few lichen species are extending their range, apparently as a result of sulphur dioxide acidifying the substrates, and could be regarded as undesirable, they are insignificant in number. There are probably few epiphytic species likely to be encountered in woodlands which could be considered to be typically non-woodland species. Species forming some associations of the alliance Xanthorion parietinae (see James, Hawksworth & Rose 1977) rarely occur in woodland and might be excluded from consideration. Care should also be taken not to make unfair comparisons between woods with differing phorophyte species. As mentioned above, species such as elm generally support a more diverse flora than, for example, beech.

Certain lichen species have been recognised by Rose (1976) as being associated with ancient and largely undisturbed woodlands. He provides a list of 30 of these species which can be used to calculate a relative index of ecological continuity (RIEC).

RIEC = (n ÷ 20) x 100, where n is the number of species in his list that occur on a site. As a result of his careful selection of species to include a range which covers the whole of the British Isles, it is hoped that this list can be used nationally. This does not, however, preclude the development of more local indices. Gilbert (1980) provides such a list for north-east England. This refinement does not greatly affect the ranking which is produced by Rose's RIEC, but helps to separate woodlands of otherwise very similar score. Bowen (1976, 1980) has produced lists for Dorset and for Berkshire, Buckinghamshire and Oxfordshire. Such indices appear to provide a simple and quick evaluation method. The lack of good historical information on which to base the selection of sites and species for these indices should not, however, be forgotten. The evaluation they provide should also be considered in conjunction with local knowledge and the total species list from a site. The presence of rare species adds importance to a site. Lichen distribution data are unfortunately not easy to obtain and hence it may not be simple to assess the rarity of a particular species. Dobson (1979) provides distribution maps for commoner species, many maps are far from complete. Watson's

(1953) Census catalogue is a useful guide, though now very much out of date. Distribution maps of a few species have been printed in the Lichenologist and various symposium volumes. Hawksworth & Seaward (1977) provide the best list of references to published work by Watsonian vice-counties. The British Lichen Society is currently mapping the distribution of all lichen species. A provisional atlas of about 100 species has been produced, with others to follow.

The most comprehensive listing of sites which are of importance for their lichen flora is found in a report by the British Lichen Society (1982), but there have been a number of subsequent changes.

Management

The current state of a wood is an expression of its management up to the time of the visit. It is not always a safe guide to future treatment, although there may be obvious trends which are unlikely to be quickly or easily reversed. The same types of management may be good or bad for nature conservation in different circumstances.

Under most types of woodland management there are often long periods when apparently little is being done and the appearance of the wood alters little. These are interspersed with periods of intense activity and often quite dramatic changes, as for example when a stand is felled and restocked. If the visit coincides with a period of activity, the wood may appear to be very heavily managed, but at another time the wood may seem to be almost neglected. An understanding of woodland management, both for commercial and conservation objectives, helps interpretation of the site as much as a knowledge of woodland ecology, and the reader may wish to consult Brooks (1980), Evans (1984), James (1982), Kirby (1984c), Peterken (1981) and Smart & Andrews (1985).

In many woods the management this century differs radically from the traditional management techniques which were widely employed from the medieval period to the late nineteenth century. Often features of nature conservation importance may best be maintained by restoring such management. Surveyors need to consider at least the past 100 years, including the depredations of two World Wars, if they are to interpret correctly the effects of past management that are reflected in the current state of the wood. Rackham (1976) is the best introduction to historical management of woodland, but shows a strong bias to eastern England. Other sources include Anderson (1967), James (1981), Leonard (1983), Linnard (1982), Rackham (1980) and Tittensor (1970).

Much of the information (Table 25) that can be collected in the field about past management comes from the woodland composition and structure – the age of the trees and shrubs, their growth form, whether they occur in straight lines or other artificial-looking patterns, whether there are species such as horse-chestnut which do not occur naturally in woods, whether the trees in a stand are of mixed or even age. An appreciation of silvicultural systems (Troup 1952; Pryor & Savill 1986) and the way that stands change in appearance at different stages in the forestry cycle may help the surveyor.

Human artefacts ranging from medieval banks to Second World War concrete rides and old bomb dumps move the story along. "Danger Fire" signs imply that the wood is probably managed for timber production; old hay bales point to pheasant-keeping being important. Heavy grazing by stock may be indicated by a short-grass-dominated ground flora and lack of understorey or regeneration, even under canopy gaps. However, the significance of grazing pressure on the woodland composition depends on the time at which it occurs, so that it is not easy to quantify its effect.

Much of the management information (particularly in Level 2 surveys) can be expressed in the form of annotated maps (see, for example, Figures 16 and 22).

Table 25   Indications of management, past and present

Possible non-woodland phase in past

Banks, buildings, internal walls or hedges, old gardens, obviously secondary woodland flora, low-branching park or wood-edge trees within the stand

Game management

"Skylights" (small holes cut in the canopy for shooting), straw bales, pheasant feeding or release areas, "cover" shrubs such as snowberry and rhododendron, cartridge cases, gibbets, old polythene sacks tied up to mark shooting points

Amenity/landscape work

Ornamental plantings of rhododendron, conifers, introduced broadleaf species often associated with rides or prominent positions

Plantation forestry

"Danger Fire" signs, remains of rabbit fences round young plantations, obvious plantations, suggestions of planting lines in old broadleaf areas especially in even-aged crops of maiden trees, a scatter of conifers through a broadleaf crop which may be the remnants of a conifer "nurse", piles of logs

Coppice/wood pasture management

Multiple stems from old coppice stools or most trees showing distinct swelling at the base indicating growth from a stool, multiple branching at about 2-3 m from a large bole (possible old pollard) (Note, however, that many wartime fellings and failed plantations have grown up as multiple stems without having been deliberately coppiced.)

Heavy grazing by stock or deer

Lack of understorey, lack of regeneration, abundance of grasses rather than herbs, signs of the animals themselves (dung, wool, etc), lack of effective fences

Soils

Soil maps at various scales are available from the Soil Survey for most of the country and may be relevant to woodland survey work. The survey and assessment of soils encounter problems similar to those found in nature conservation surveys, notably the need to extrapolate from a limited number of physical parameters which can be examined easily to the broader issue of soil suitability for particular crops. Proper soil surveys are carried out by exposing soil profiles in pits and by augur samples. These methods are described in the publications of the Soil Survey of England and Wales. For a general introduction to soil, see White (1979) or Russell (1973), although the latter is somewhat out-of-date in parts. The NCC generally has taken only limited interest in soils, whether as part of its survey work or in terms of overall conservation strategy, but Ball & Stevens (1981) assess the value of ancient woodland sites in conserving undisturbed soil profiles.

Soil characteristics play a part in Peterken's Stand Type classification, and there is generally a strong correlation between different vegetation types and soil conditions in other classification systems. However, the comments about soils in survey reports are often inferred by the surveyor from a knowledge of the vegetation. Ratcliffe (1977) provides a summary of the broad response of plants to woodland soil and climatic conditions, and more detail for particular species is given by Peterken (1981) and Rackham (1975, 1980).

It is not practicable to consider digging a full-sized soil pit in Level 2 surveys. Occasional auguring and examination of the soil in natural exposures (ditches, rabbit-holes etc.) is sometimes possible, as is a look at the surface layers in a shallow hole dug by trowel. Small samples may be taken for subsequent pH measurement, but surveyors should be aware that these may vary very widely within a short distance even in apparently uniform soils, and little emphasis should be placed on small differences between samples.

Texture

Texture refers to the relative amounts of sand, silt and clay particles in the soil. These are characterised by the following properties.

Sand   -   Individual grains can be clearly seen or felt. Soil mass feels gritty and is usually loose. Not sticky or plastic.

Silt   -   Individual particles too small to be seen or felt. Sample when moist can be moulded but will not form a thin flexible "ribbon" of soil material. Does not feel noticeably sticky but has a marked soapy or slippery feel.

Clay   -   Individual particles are even finer. When dry usually forms very hard lumps. Is quite plastic when wet and will form a long thin flexible "ribbon" when pressed between thumb and forefinger. Sticky and cohesive.

A high organic content makes clay soils less sticky and sandy soils feel more silty. "Heavy" soils are those with a high clay or silt content. "Light" soils are those with a high sand content. (The terms are derived from the effort needed to pull implements through the soil.)

Texture is assessed by thoroughly moistening a soil sample and working it with the fingers to break down the soil aggregates. A simple "key" is given in Table 26. At least distinguish soils with a significant clay content (sticky) from predominantly sandy (gritty) or silty (soapy or slippery) soils. Where there is a pronounced organic layer, record the texture of this as fibrous, granular or amorphous. Record the presence of stones in the profile.

Table 26   Texture assessment in soils

Moisten soil till it just glistens when thoroughly worked. (Jif lemons are useful for carrying water; otherwise spit.)
Roll the worked moist soil into a thin worm about 3-4 mm in diameter, about 4" long and coil it into a ring.

1a.	Neither ring nor worm formed) Fragile worm, no ring) Weak worm, feeble ring)	**Sand**	Gritty soils which when dry are usually loose or only very slightly coherent. Individual soil particules can be clearly seen with the eye or hand lens.
1b.	Worm formed; ring may be cracked, slightly sticky	**Loam**	Soil does not feel predominantly sticky, gritty or slippery. When moist it moulds readily and forms moderately coherent balls of friable soil material. Wet soil slightly sticky and plastic; dry material usually soft.
1c.	Coherent worm and ring	Go to 2.	
2a.	Sand dominant or highly noticeable: Moderately sticky Very sticky and plastic when wet	**Sandy clay loam** **Sandy clay**	Dominant feeling of stickiness but also significantly gritty.
2b.	Some sand present (not significant): Moderately sticky Only slightly sticky, slippery	**Clay loam** **(Silt loam)**	Clay and clay loam (not silt loam: see below) have dominant feeling of stickiness without any grittiness or silkiness.
2c.	Sand virtually absent	Go to 3.	
3a.	Extremely sticky and plastic, not slippery or silky	**Clay**	Soils which are sticky and plastic when wet and usually hard when dry. When moist soil is pressed between thumb and forefinger it will give a polished surface and can be drawn out to form a ribbon (excluding silt loam).
3b.	Predominantly sticky, but significantly slippery or silky: Very sticky and plastic Moderately sticky and plastic	**Silty clay** **Silty clay loam**	Dominant feeling of stickiness but also significantly slippery or silky.
3c.	Not or only very slightly sticky: Soapy or silky feeling noticeable Soapy or sily feeling dominant	**Silt loam** **Silt**	Soils which have a soft soapy or slippery feel. When moist soil is pressed between thumb and forefinger it will not give a polished appearance or be drawn out into a flexible ribbon but will give a broken furrowed appearance.

Structure

Structure refers to the way in which the basic soil particles (sand, silt, clay) are aggregated into relatively permanent "peds" separated by natural planes of weakness. Dig at the profile with a penknife and break up clods with the fingers. Distinguish the following four conditions.

(a) Aggregates (peds) less than 1 cm diameter - granular or crumb-like

(b) Aggregates (peds) usually several centimetres across - blocky, platy, prismatic

(c) Soil particles stick together but without recognisable planes of weakness (usually high clay content) - massive

(d) Soil particles show virtually no cohesion (like sand on beach) - single-grained

Topsoil is usually granular or crumb-like. The aggregates are irregularly rounded with numerous spaces between them. Granules are relatively hard and non-porous. Crumbs are soft and porous. Blocky, prismatic and platy structures are more likely in the lower rather than the upper parts of the soil and where there is a high clay content. The aggregates are close-fitting. The main differences between the three types are that the horizontal axis is greater than the vertical axis for platy structures and vice versa for prismatic ones, while with blocky structures the two axes are about equal. The structure may be described as weakly or strongly developed, according to the distinctness of the individual aggregates and the ease with which they are broken down to the basic mineral particles. Do not mistake temporary clods, as thrown up by digging, for the structural units.

Drainage

If water replaces air in the soil pores, anaerobic conditions develop. Ferric iron compounds (which are responsible for much of the orange-red-brown colour of mineral soil) are reduced to blue-grey-green ferrous ones. This and other changes associated with waterlogging are known as gleying. If the waterlogging is only temporary, some of the ferrous compounds are subsequently reoxidised. This takes place more easily in some parts of the soil than in others and produces "mottling". When the soil aggregates (crumbs etc) are broken open, alternate spots of orange-red-brown ferric compounds and blue-grey-green ferrous compounds are seen. Orange mottling may also occur along roots.

(a) No mottling or gleying in top 30 cm; soil dry or damp to feel (except after rain) - freely drained

(b) Signs of mottling in top 30 cm; may be gleying below 30 cm; soil dry or wet - poorly drained

(c) Signs of gleying (and mottling) in top 30 cm; soil more or less permanently wet; a dark peaty layer often present at the surface - waterlogged (very poorly drained)

Freely drained conditions are more likely where the soil has a high sand or stone content or well mixed-in organic matter or a strongly developed crumb or granular structure. Upper slopes and plateaux are more likely to be freely drained than lower slopes and valley bottoms provided that there are no impervious layers which prevent free movement of water.

Poor drainage (and waterlogged) conditions are more likely to develop:

(a)   in valley bottoms where the water table is close to the surface;

(b)   on lower slopes which are receiving large amounts of water from higher up;

(c)   on upper slopes or plateaux where downward water movement is restricted by iron pans, clay or peat layers; (The higher the rainfall, the more likely it is that the water will not be able to drain away fast enough, leading to anaerobic conditions.)

(d)   in "flushed" zones along streams or by springs where there is lateral movement of water from elsewhere.

If poor drainage or waterlogging occurs, indicate which if any of the above conditions appears to fit the site.

pH

If a pH meter is available, take a sample of soil (about three tablespoons full) from 10-15 cm depth for subsequent pH determination. Put the sample in a polythene bag or tin. Make sure it is well labelled.

Organic horizons

O   –   peaty, wet for most of the year

L   –   undecomposed litter

F   –   partly decomposed litter

H   –   well decomposed humus layer, low mineral content, plant remains unrecognisable

L, F and H horizons occur where the organic matter is not wet for most of the year.

Below these there may be a mixed organic matter—mineral soil (A) layer which is black or dark brown in colour, becoming paler and more red-brown with depth as the organic matter content decreases. Alternatively there may be a relatively sharp transition, with the mineral soil much paler than the organic matter above it, and in extreme cases the mineral soil may consist of bleached grey sand (E horizon).

Distinguish the following types of organic matter content and record the approximate depth of the layers.

(a)   Relatively thin (few cm) purely organic layer; little distinction between L, F and H layers, which merge into mineral soil below. Well-developed mixed organic matter—mineral soil (A) layer.

Mull

(b)   Organic layer well-developed; may be quite deep in conifer stands, but not wet and peaty. There may be sharp transitions between layers within the organic layer and to the mineral soil. Mixed organic matter—mineral soil (A) layer thin or absent.

Mor

(c)   Intermediate between above. Upper organic layers well developed, but greater mixing of organic matter and mineral soil.

Moder

(d)   Organic layer well developed, peaty; virtually no mixing with mineral soil. May be very deep. Wet for most of year.

Peat

Mull humus forms on soils of moderate to high base status. The mixing with the mineral soil is caused by earthworms. The composition of the litter is important. Mull humus is associated with grassland and much deciduous woodland. Mor humus is more common on base-poor soils and under heathland or conifers, but these differences are not absolute.

Soil mineral layers

Below the purely organic layers the following mixed organic—mineral or pure mineral horizons occur.

(a)   Dark-coloured (black or dark brown), becoming paler with depth; often granular or crumb-like; mixed organic matter—mineral soil.   **A (A_1 in earlier systems)**

(b)   Paler (in extreme cases bleached sand); no organic matter present; often only weakly structured.   **E (A_2 in earlier systems)**

A well-developed A horizon is a characteristic of mull humus conditions. The E (eluvial) layer may be present below the A horizon. Under peat or mor humus it may be directly below the organic layer. Clay minerals and sesquioxides are removed from this layer; hence its pale colour and poor structure. Record whether A and E horizons are visible in the top 30 cm of soil and their approximate depth. Below the A or, where present, the E horizon is the B horizon, which consists of weathered parent material enriched by material from above. This is the zone of maximum clay accumulation and consequently often has a blocky, platy or prismatic structure. Iron removed from the E layer is also deposited here and may give rise to an iron pan which impedes drainage. (A narrow band of humic material may be deposited with the iron.)

Often only the top of the B horizon will be present in the top 30 cm (sometimes not even that). Occasionally the parent material - the C horizon - is reached. This may be derived from the underlying rock, or the soil may be formed on material transported from elsewhere, e.g. glacial till or recent alluvium. Record the characteristics of the B and C horizons if these are visible.

<u>Soil classification</u> (after Curtis, Courtney & Trudgill 1976; Burnham 1980)

Seven major groups of soils are recognised, each of which is further subdivided. In most cases it ought to be possible to assign a soil sample to one of these major groups in the field. Occasionally it will be possible to be more precise.

1	Thick man-made topsoil or disturbed soil more than 40 cm deep, e.g. areas with long history of cultivation, spoil-heaps.	Man-made soils
2	Surface peat horizon more than 40 cm thick, formed under wet conditions.	Peat soils
3	Bedrock or little altered unconsolidated parent material (e.g. sand in sand-dune successions) at 30 cm depth or less. Within this major group are included rendzinas, derived from very calcareous material, and rankers, where the topsoil is non-calcareous.	Lithomorphic soils
4	Distinct mixed organic--mineral (A) horizon or peaty (O) horizon over grey or grey and brown mottled sub-surface horizon. Evidence of gleying in top 30 cm. Periodic or permanent waterlogging.	Gley soils
5	Pale E (A_2) horizon (which may be bleached). Below this is a black or brown layer in upper B horizon caused by accumulation of iron or aluminium in amorphous forms associated with organic matter. Usually under mor humus or peaty horizons. Mixed organic--mineral (A) layer poorly developed or absent. Well drained to poorly drained.	Podzolic soils
6	Well-developed mixed organic--mineral (A) horizon (usually with mull or moder humus) with brownish sub-surface (B) horizon. Common under deciduous woodland and grassland over much of Britain. This group includes brown earths proper, as well as similar soils developed on sand or alluvium, but excludes pelosols (see below).	Brown soils
7	Slowly permeable non-alluvial soils that crack deeply in dry seasons, with brown, greyish or reddish, blocky or prismatic sub-surface (B) horizons. Usually slightly mottled (some restriction of drainage). No E (eluvial) horizon.	Pelosols

Guidelines for soil recording for woodland surveyors

Dig a hole 25-30 cm deep with a trowel. A penknife is useful for cutting roots. Keep one side vertical - the "profile". Make a brief description of the soil properties exhibited by this profile along the lines of the example given below. Make sure the pit is filled before you leave. The aim is not the full description of a soil scientist (who normally goes to 1 m + depth) but to concentrate on the physical features which are likely to have the greatest ecological significance - texture, drainage, pH (base status), organic matter. More detail is provided by Hodgson (1974).

A simple soil description might be:

L, F, H horizons 1 cm, mixed tree (oak, ash) and grass litter.

A   1-3 cm   Dark brown sandy loam, with weak crumb structure, showing
B   3-25 cm   gradual transition to light brown B horizon; small stones
                   present throughout.

Mull humus. Freely drained, base of slope. pH 5.5. Brown soil.

Soil surface features (C Ranson)

Included in this section are both natural surface features, such as periglacial depressions, and man-made ones such as banks or ditches (Figure 28). Such features, where they can be identified, provide information on the history of the woodland and help explain some of the patterns in plant communities within a site (Rackham 1976, 1980, 1986a; Peterken 1981).

Screes and landslips

Surface movement occurs on cliffs, on steep slopes or in layered strata, or where high water content renders rocks, soil, subsoil or even base-rock mobile. Extreme forms are the screes with sparse tree cover of the Peak and Lake Districts and the densely vegetated "flows" of clays in South Essex and the Weald. Sometimes the movement is catastrophic: more commonly it is continuous slow movement. Movement presents opportunities for tree colonisation, changes in drainage and water status and physical and chemical changes in soils.

Surface depressions

The land surface of lowland Britain is not smooth; among the most widespread features creating minor irregularities are the numerous depressions, often more or less circular or elongate, between 5 and 45 m across. Early large-scale maps, and especially the first edition of the Ordance Survey 25" to 1 mile maps, show great numbers of depressions, often water-filled. They are frequent on farmland, but usually denser in ancient woodland, and it is tempting to suggest that woodland ponds, and most non-woodland ponds, are of natural origin. Rackham (1980) describes ponds and pond-pairs in many woods of eastern England. Parts of east Suffolk, for example farmland between Beccles and Halesworth, still have a high density of ponds, including pairs and triplets. The ponds have no upcast, display an irregular outline and depth and are most frequent on level ground. They probably arose from the melting of ground-ice at the end of the last cold phase of the Ice Age.

Springs

The geology of woods is often complex. One aspect of this is the frequent occurrence of springs rising in woods and, before leaving the wood, providing water for ponds and marshes. Often the marsh is so wet that no woody growth casts shade on it, but misguided attempts to drain springs, ponds and marshes often lead to a stagnant, shady bog.

Loess, cover-sands and sand lenses

During the last cold phase of the Ice Age, strong and persistent easterly winds blew round the continental high pressure system. They brought fine sand, silt and some clay from central and northern Europe into western Europe. In the British Isles, the main distribution of wind-blown deposits lies in East Anglia, Kent and the southern coastal counties and to the east of the Pennines. Locally, the amount of wind-blown material in the topsoil varies from none to a blanket many feet thick. While pure loess produces a very fertile soil, the more sandy variants are relatively poor in nutrients and the soils are very acidic (down to pH 3.3). Only where the winds formed sand-dunes or lenses of sand do the sands have an effect on the topography; weathering has reduced their height but they still have domed surfaces. In spite of being sandy they hold water and discharge it only slowly during summer; this may be aided by the peat content in the dense bracken litter in the top foot or so. The bracken effectively prevents colonisation by woody shrubs, except locally where rabbits and badgers break through and allow alder, hazel and birch to establish themselves.

Figure 28   Earthworks in a wood (Peterken 1981: reproduced by permission of the author)

Plan of earthworks in Overhall Grove, Cambs.   Beneath the wood lie the remains of a moated manor house site within a multiply-banked enclosure.   There are also remains of fishponds, field boundary banks and ridge-and-furrow cultivation.   The woodland edge is not defined by a large wood bank.

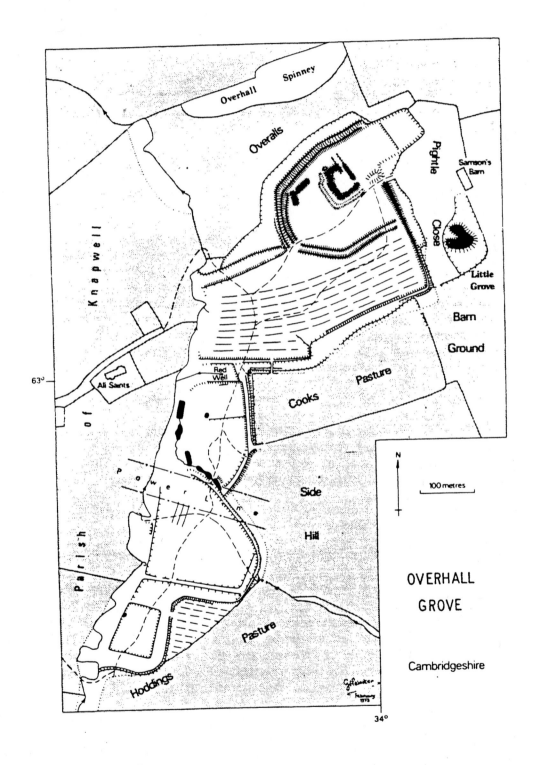

To summarise, the chief charactistics of sand lenses are a wet, treeless area of an acre or more, a dense cover of bracken, few trees and shrubs (mainly hazel, birch and alder), bluebells on and near the margins, and a peripheral discharge of water.

Drainage patterns

Certain woodland surfaces, especially those with a high loess content in the upper 50 cm, have intricate dendritic drainage systems. They are not man-made, but the fossilised drainage patterns from the Late-Glacial stage of the last cold phase of the Ice Age. Many of them still carry water in winter, though others have been interrupted by wood banks and rides.

Roads and tracks

Although some present-day roads and tracks in woods may be the successors of animal tracks in Wildwood times, most are known, from documentary and archaeological evidence, to be man-made. In lowland Britain woods are often subdivided by rides that have been used for vehicular access for the last 300 to 400 years. Before that, access and management were often by foot, using a dense network of narrow footpaths.

Boundaries

One of the distinctive features of woods is their boundaries. They are usually artificial in some way or other, particularly in the lowlands, and they rarely grade "naturally" into some other type of vegetation or land-use; the chief exception is secondary woodland colonising open ground.

Woods may be confined by streams, ditches and banks, hedges, pales, walls and stone slabs. As a rule, the more sinuous or the larger the structure defining the wood, the older it is, although there must be exceptions, especially where insubstantial Iron Age and Roman features form the wood margin and where deer have been kept. In lowland England pollards, often of oak, ash, elm and maple, grow on wood boundaries. Many of them are over 500 years old judged by their size, and they give a rough minimum date to the definition of a particular wood. Sometimes details of management, descriptions of perambulations or early maps (pre-1620) will give a minimum age for an existing wood boundary or confirm a later reduction. Another characteristic of ditch and bank boundaries is the relatively base-rich subsoil that will have been thrown up; such woody species as spindle, dogwood, maple and privet tend to grow there even if they are absent in the body of the wood. Other wood-edge species, present because of birds rather than soil characteristics, are holly, guelder-rose, wayfaring-tree, wild service tree and crab apple.

Former deer-parks dominated by woodland have specially constructed wood banks and had launds for grazing. The launds were defined by ditches and banks making a rough square or irregular oval of one to five acres. Many of the surviving launds have now become secondary woodland, but their sites can be identified.

Ditches and banks inside woods

Many woods have been subdivided during their history, possibly because of change of ownership or because new ways of managing the wood were introduced, resulting in separately-named adjoining woods with a common ditch and bank. These ditches and banks vary in size from modest and straight to massive and sinuous with ponds and hollows.

Field systems

Iron Age field systems within ancient woodland of medieval or greater age occur in central and southern Essex, and archaeologists have demonstrated extensive pre-Roman, Roman and early Anglo-Saxon occupation of land which has been woodland for a very long time. Systematic survey by archaeologists of the more extensive tracts of woodland elsewhere in lowland Britain may show this phenomenon to be fairly common.

At the other end of the time-scale, the 25" to 1 mile Ordnance Survey of c. 1895–1905 shows fields of grass or arable where now there is woodland. Often the former hedges and ditches or walls can still be recognised.

Plotland

In Kent, Essex, Hertfordshire and Cambridgeshire (and possibly elsewhere), there are tracts of land (10–1,000 acres) which were converted from woodland and farmland to low-grade housing between 1880 and 1930 – a period of low agricultural activity. Conversion was never total. Remnants of ancient woodland and farmland survived among the houses and bungalows. Much plotland has now become secondary woodland.

Houses, gardens and working sites

The name "Woodhouse" occurs frequently in place-names and surnames. Many woods have extant or former houses in them. The curtilage of the house often includes a fenced boundary ditch and bank surrounding the garden (up to one acre or more), a well and an access track. Each might have had a yard for storing and converting produce out in the wood. Charcoal pits and hearths are frequent in the woods of some counties, especially in the north-west, the West Midlands and southern England. These sites have usually reverted to secondary woodland and can be recognised by their earthworks, remains of brick- and timber-work, dilapidated outhouses, well-heads, fruit trees, and elders and nettles.

Mineral workings

Until recent decades minerals were taken from the ground and the holes left to regenerate with whatever colonised the ground. The minerals dug from the ground varied from coal and limestone to clay and peat. These workings had little by way of soil, so that there is now extensive secondary woodland on all these substrates. The age of this woodland ranges from 10-12-year-old birch-sallow scrub on wet sand and gravel-pit floors, through 200-year-old alder carr, to ash woods on limestone screes of Roman origin.

Monitoring

Introduction

Monitoring is used here to mean the detection and measurement of change through repeated surveys over time. A fuller discussion on monitoring in general is given by Burn (1986) and by Smith, Wells & Welsh (1985). In theory, any set of survey results could form the basis for subsequent monitoring. However, changes over time cannot be detected until they are greater than the level of variation inherent in the first survey. Therefore monitoring is usually carried out to a higher level of detail and precision than ordinary Level 2 surveys.

There are two main situations in which monitoring may be considered appropriate. The first is where some change is expected to take place in a particular area as a result of management decisions, e.g. the invasion by trees of grassland after a reduction in grazing or the change in the ground flora after the felling of a wood. The areas affected and the likely changes are known, and the samples should be taken in the most efficient way to measure the expected change. Although measurements of the changes in any plot over time may be interesting, they will be more useful (a) if the state of the area before the change is known and (b) if comparable control areas are also recorded (Figure 29).

Figure 29   Monitoring changes after felling, using permanent plots

A series of permanent 10 x 10 m quadrats were set up in 1984 in Sheephouse Wood (Bucks), in areas subject to different treatments. The subsequent changes in species numbers are shown for an unfelled plot (●), a plot felled in the winter of 1983 (O), a plot where the understorey but not the overstorey was cut in 1983 (△) and a plot felled in the winter of 1985 (■).

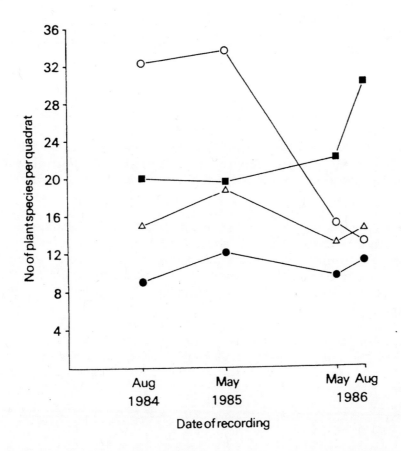

The second situation arises where it is intended to monitor change over a large area, some parts of which may change during the period concerned, but it is impossible to say where such change may occur or what it will be. Dawkins & Field (1978) conclude that for this purpose a combination of a systematic distribution of samples and of selected samples chosen to be typical of particular areas is the best solution.

If the expected changes are large, a series of random or stratified random samples may have a low enough standard error to remove the necessity for rerecording precisely the same ground. However, monitoring schemes usually depend on revisiting precisely the same area and rerecording the plot, transect or photographic point either in precisely the same way or in such a way that any methodological differences can be allowed for, because this increases the chances that change will be detected. Three things are crucial:

(a)   precise description and marking of the plots;

(b)   precise recording of the methods used;

(c)   careful storage and retrieval of the original data.

The longer the scheme is intended to run, the more important these become, since the original recorder (and his or her memory of what was done) may no longer be available. Recently a register of permanent vegetation plots has been created (Hill & Radford 1986).

Suitable permanent markers may range from wooden pegs or marks on trees or rocks for short-term projects to large posts, buried metal rods or angle-irons for longer ones. Markers must be easy to find by those who know where they are (roughly), but not so conspicuous that vandals or others remove them. Also, if they are too conspicuous, curious visitors frequently go over to see what they are and so disturb the area excessively. Indeed there is always the risk that the permanent plots or their surroundings will be affected by the recording process itself. This is very apparent in some grassland studies.

Plots and transects

Monitoring studies to detect some (unspecified) future change and based on systematic grids of quadrats include those of Sykes (1976), Horrill & Sykes (1975, 1976, 1977) and Dawkins & Field (1978). Because most of these were set up relatively recently, they have usually not had their first rerecording. Results from a partial resurvey of quadrats in Wytham Wood have been given earlier (Figure 24; Horsfall & Kirby 1985).

As an alternative to quadrats, Peterken & Jones (1987) and Peterken & Stace (1987) describe a system of transects established in Lady Park Wood (Gloucs) and in the Black Wood of Rannoch (Perthshire) which show long-term changes in unmanaged woodland (see also Figure 23). Similar transects are being or have been established in a number of other sites to study natural forest disturbance patterns in Britain (Backmeroff 1987). Transects are often easier to mark and refind than quadrats, but they restrict the area that can be sampled.

One of the commonest types of monitoring in relation to a particular issue has been of regeneration and the response of the ground flora to changes in grazing (for example Pigott 1983; Sykes & Horrill 1985), and some recent results from Cumbria are given in Table 27.

By contrast, long-term monitoring of the changes under commercial forestry management seem to be relatively scarce (Hill & Jones 1978; Ovington 1955; Anderson 1979), although there appear to be no real problems preventing the establishment of such schemes.

Other long-term monitoring studies include the work of Tamm (1956), Falinski (1986), Leemans (1986), Bucking (1986) and Bucking et al. (1986).

Table 27   Regeneration survey in eight-year-old enclosures at Great Wood, Borrowdale (Cumbria) (data supplied by N A Robinson)

Regeneration was recorded in transects 2 m wide and 20 m apart, to give a sample of about 10% of the total area, by using height classes marked on a cane (see below for the classes used). The class TN covers any gap between the top of the regeneration scale (5 m) and the bottom of the scale used in a separate tree enumeration. The centre line of the transect was marked by a plastic line, and a cane with 1 m marked on either side of the line was moved forward about 1 m at a time, so that the search area was a 1 x 1 m square on each side of the line at a time. Seedlings less than 10 cm high were ignored. The ends of each transect were marked by plastic ties on the fence, with additional marker posts put in to provide a mid-point for long transects. The examples from the results given below have been converted to seedling numbers per hectare. For comparison, 1,100 trees per ha is roughly equivalent to 3 m between seedlings or saplings.

Species	Regeneration height class						
	1	2	3	4	5	TN	Total
Ash	3775	1884	685	395	156	30	6925
Sycamore	1772	141	45	22			1980
Elm	97	82	82	74			335
Hawthorn	89	74	67	15	30		275
Hazel	22	52	60	45	7		186
Holly	15	37	74	22	15		163
Birch	127	15	15				157
Oak	15	60	45	7			127
Willow					15		15
Alder					7		7

Regeneration height classes: 1 = 10–25 cm, 2 = 26–50 cm, 3 = 51–100 cm, 4 = 101–200 cm, 5 = 201–500 cm, TN = stem more than 500 cm high but less than 7.5 cm diameter (breast height).

Photographic monitoring

Establishment of fixed-point systems for photographic monitoring is described in Nature Conservancy Council (1978), and the potential value of photographs is illustrated by the changes recorded at Wistmans Wood, Devon (Proctor, Spooner & Spooner 1980). Changes in the canopy at Madingley Wood, Cambridgeshire, over time have been recorded by a series of photographs taken with a "fish-eye" hemispherical lens (D A Coombe pers. comm.). Experiments have also been done with photographic recording of epiphytic lichen and bryophyte communities with a view to long-term monitoring (information supplied by N A Robinson).

In May 1986 photographs were taken of <u>Lobaria</u> colonies on important lichen-bearing trees in Great Wood, Borrowdale (Cumbria). The object was not to record accurately the growth or otherwise of individual thalli, which would require a large number of close-up photographs taken under standardised conditions, but to take a smaller number of photographs showing representative areas of trunks from which it would be possible to see quite readily how the lichens were faring and in particular whether thalli were dropping off (or being knocked off by squirrels), as appeared to be the case in some instances, and whether they were being replaced by new growth. The trees photographed were marked on a map.

The area of trunk being photographed was marked by drilling holes <u>c</u>. 2 cm deep into the bark and inserting the smallest size of white cylindrical "Plasplug", which was clipped off so as to project just enough beyond the surface to make it visible and not readily overgrown by mosses. Numbered large-headed map pins were pushed into the Plasplugs while the photographs were being taken and thus appeared in the corners of the frames. Unfortunately some of the numbers cannot be read, as the white surface caused over-exposure. A Minolta 300 camera with 35-70 mm Tamron lens was mounted on a Geant tripod. The film was Kodacolor 200, from which standard matt-finish enprints were obtained. Colour print film was used instead of transparencies for ease of subsequent comparison in the field. A focal length of 70 mm was used, taking advantage of the "macro" facility which enabled the tripod to be placed away from tree roots. With an aperture of f 22 to obtain maximum depth of field, speeds on automatic setting were often ¼-1 second, so a cable release was used to avoid vibration; the sliding cap provided was used to cover the viewfinder after focussing to keep stray light off the internal meter. The photographs were taken in horizontal format, usually covering the width of the tree, in a series upwards to head height, after which the camera was tilted to take a last shot up the trunk with the top markers in the bottom corners. In some cases general shots were also taken to show all the markers in position and surrounding foliage. Wherever possible, the photographs were taken with cloud over the sun to avoid contrasts of illumination on the trunks and strong shadows, which alter the appearance of lichens. Thirty-seven photographs were taken in two days of work and the cost of film and processing was about £10.

The system worked as intended and the photographs were sharply in focus, showing that at f 22 it is possible to cope with the irregularities and curvature of trunks. The quality of the standard enprints was perfectly satisfactory for the initial purposes, and enlargements can be made if it is subsequently required to make comparisons of particular shots. Data sheets have been prepared logging the details of the photographs for each tree, and these are stored with the film and prints in the file.

<u>Rare plant monitoring</u> (L Farrell)

The following methods are recommended for recording changes in the populations of particular species.

Taping

Select the study area. Drive in 2.5 cm x 2.5 cm x 30 cm hardwood pegs to ground level at regular intervals, no more than 5 m apart. Locate and map the positions of these pegs accurately in relation to the topography. Screw a brass cup-hook into the top of each peg. These pegs then form the permanent reference points. The cup-hooks are removed after recording. Attach two 30 m tape measures to adjacent cup-hooks. Record measurements from these two permanent reference points to an individual plant or clone. This defines the plant's or clone's position by a unique pair of co-ordinates. Repeat the process for each individual in the population (or part of the population) which is to be mapped. Record any other characteristics which may be required, e.g. number of flowers, height of inflorescence, number of leaves, health and seed production.

Fixed quadrat

This is probably a better method for assessing a population where individuals grow very close together. It is based on a 1 m² quadrat and is essentially the same method as is used in National Grid References.

Lay the quadrat, which should have at least two sides marked off in centimetres, over the selected study area. Mark each corner by driving hardwood pegs in to ground level. Using a ruler or bicycle spoke, make right-angled lines from an individual plant to the two measuring scales and read off the distances from the corner of the quadrat. Record any other relevant details. Repeat the process until all individuals within the 1 m² are recorded. Selected or random quadrats can be used throughout the population. If the population is large, take a small sample, as detailed recording is time-consuming and a relatively quick method is needed for regular monitoring.

These two methods work well where the ground is firm, but in wet habitats the pegs will slowly sink. If the pegs are capped with metal and they have not sunk further than 15 cm, they can be located by means of a metal-detector. If the ground is not in any way firm, use will have to be made of natural features such as rocks or trees. In a barren landscape (such as a bog), orienteering methods will have to be employed.

Other types of monitoring

Reference has been made in other sections to butterfly monitoring, bird population monitoring using the Common Birds Census and the monitoring of landscape change. Systems for recording change on nature reserves, such as the event record system (Peterken 1969) and its successors, provide a general means of investigating changes over time on particular sites.

Conclusions

Monitoring studies can be very valuable, but those setting up the baseline should consider carefully:

(a)   whether the records collected initially are of value in their own right even if no further recordings are done;

(b)   whether the system is one which can survive five, 10 or even more years of neglect and still be retrievable.

The original descriptions should be as detailed as possible but allow for subsequent recordings to be simpler. The setting-up of permanent plots or transects can be an expensive exercise and consequently requires careful planning to ensure that the right areas are chosen and the right things are measured.

Publication and publicity

Survey results are of no value unless they are used. Survey methods and results should be properly written up and made available to as wide a range of people and organisations as possible; see, for example, Rackham (1986b) and Colebourn (1983). Often this aspect is neglected and even the fact that the survey took place may be forgotten.

The field records, supplemented by written site reports, constitute the basic results. Copies should be sent to owners and managers, partly as a matter of courtesy but also because they cannot take account of nature conservation unless they are provided with the necessary information. Unless there are problems of confidentiality, the following bodies are likely to be able to use, and hence may want, the basic results - the NCC, the Forestry Commission, the local authority and the local Conservation or Wildlife Trust.

With larger surveys in particular, it is desirable to produce a report describing the survey, how it was organised, the methods used, problems encountered, the woods surveyed and the results. The results might include description of the main vegetation types found, the woodland management, the distribution of species and some evaluation of the results in nature conservation terms. Recommendations for further work or survey are helpful. It is best if those who did the survey can also write the report, as they are likely to be able to include details which may not be obvious from the basic site records. The report can and should have a wider circulation than the basic site records. The more attractive and "professional-looking" the report, the more likely people are to take notice of what it contains; so care in the preparation and presentation of the data is usually worthwhile.

Most survey results and reports are not "published" in the formal sense. People outside the immediate area, in geographical or subject terms, may not know that a survey has taken place and are unlikely to pick it up through the normal procedures of literature searching or following up references. Even within the area, there is always a risk that once those immediately involved with the survey have moved on the results will be forgotten or buried in some obscure file. The development of local Biological Record Centres and of local and national data-banks can help to overcome this problem, and survey results should be made available to these where appropriate. Permanent plots should be recorded on the register being developed by Hill & Radford (1986). Often, however, the best way to ensure that a survey is known about is to prepare part of the results for "formal" publication in a journal, whether local or national. This will lead the interested reader back to the full report and thence, if necessary, to the basic records.

Various attempts have been made within the NCC to prepare an index of existing surveys, but this is still an area where improvement is needed. The examples given within this book do no more than indicate a small part of the material that is already available. There are many woods still to be surveyed, but we are building on an already extensive framework of knowledge. I hope this book will contribute to that framework.

Appendices 1–4

Woodland evaluation

General hints on survey organisation

Recording forms and instructions

Main classification systems

Appendix 1: Woodland evaluation

Woodland evaluation is discussed in more detail in Game & Peterken (1984), Goodfellow & Peterken (1981), Kirby (1980, 1986), Peterken (1981) and Ratcliffe (1977), but a summary of some of the points covered in these is given below. It is assumed that evaluation will be based on results from a Level 2 survey so that the woods can be compared in terms of at least some of the woodland features listed in Table 5.

Evaluations should be made as systematic as possible. Initially the interest of sites or sub-sites is broken down and they are compared for each feature in turn, if possible in a quantitative way. This last is fairly straightforward for size, numbers of species or the presence or absence of rarities, but is much more difficult to do in a meaningful way for a feature such as structure.

These different features do not all have equal significance for nature conservation; indeed several are only important when viewed in conjunction with others. The more that are considered, the better will be the overall assessment of value. Attempts have been made to devise "combined scores" for all the features recorded (but not necessarily for all that are important on a site), so that comparisons between sites can be made simply on the basis of such combined scores. There are theoretical and practical objections to such an approach and at present it appears to be more useful to accept that there are limits to quantification and that value judgements at some stage cannot be avoided.

Nature conservation objectives will vary to some extent according to the people and woods concerned, so that differing priorities may for example be given to relative naturalness of a site as opposed to its overall species-richness or to richness for birds as against vascular plants. The particular peculiarities of each survey must also be borne in mind when deciding how the results can be used. It is therefore impossible to specify a single evaluation procedure, but the framework in Table 28 overleaf may be helpful.

The assessment stages A-G do not have to be taken in the order given, and some may be left out (as the information may not be available or relevant) or others may be added. At any stage a wood may be judged to be sufficiently good (X) or sufficiently bad (Y) for one or a combination of features as to make further consideration unnecessary; for example it may be judged to be important on its rarity score alone.

110

Table 28   A framework for woodland evaluation   (See text for explanation.)

Survey results for a group of woods

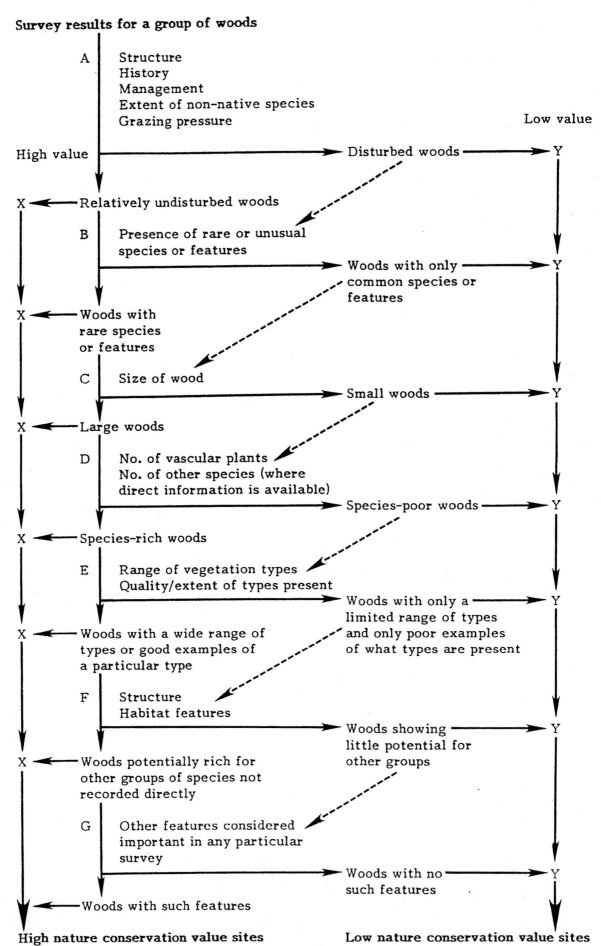

High nature conservation value sites   Low nature conservation value sites

Appendix 2: General hints on survey organisation

Timing

The field survey work is best done between the second half of April and late August or early September, with the May-June period as the best overall time. Ideally all preparatory work should have been done before then, in particular preparing a list of sites and obtaining permission to survey them. Much time will be wasted by the surveyors otherwise. If the results are to be written up properly, this could require a further one or two months at the end of four or five months' fieldwork. Winter surveys can provide some information and are particularly useful for studies of surface features such as banks, tree distribution, structure and lower plants.

Selection of sites for survey

If the aim is to collect information on the "best" sites for nature conservation, the selection of sites may be based on size, history, composition, results of a Level 1 survey, sites missed from previous surveys, etc. For logistical reasons it may be helpful to group woods which are close together or which have easy access. On other occasions it may be important to survey sites across the range of size classes, ownerships or geology within a county. Site selection should be done before the survey starts. Enough sites should be selected to allow for substitutes in case access proves impossible on some or survey proves faster than expected. Allow for rainy days however. It is easy to overestimate how much can be achieved: one or two woods per field day is about the best that can be maintained.

Access

It is the joint responsibility of the organiser of the survey and the surveyors to ensure that permission has been given for a wood to be surveyed. Parish councils, local National Farmers' Union, Country Landowners Association, Timber Growers UK, Forestry Commission and Conservation and Wildlife Trusts may be able to help by suggesting who should be contacted about a site. If all these sources fail one can ask at the nearest farm. However, often a written request to the owner is required; there may be shooting tenants and gamekeepers to be informed. Surveyors should not be expected to get permission and survey the wood on the same day. In addition, it is often better if the survey organiser, rather than the surveyors, arranges access, because he or she is more likely to be able to answer questions about why the survey is being done or what the results will be used for. I recommend starting to request access permission at least a month or two before the surveyors are due to start.

Methods

The choice of methods depends on the objectives. I hope this book provides some guidance! Once the methods have been decided, they should be tested by the survey organiser in both easy and difficult situations, especially if he or she will not be taking part in the survey work proper.

Training

Time spent at the start of the survey in familiarisation with the method and standardisation of how different features are to be recorded is seldom wasted. For surveys of more than two months a period of at least a week should be assigned to this. It may help to visit as wide a range of sites as possible in this time so that the surveyors have a better idea what sort of conditions they can expect. Obviously the more experienced the surveyors, the less training will be required. However well the initial training and survey has gone, the methods and surveyors' experiences should be reviewed from time to time to ensure that the standard of survey remains consistent.

Single surveyors or survey teams

It is possible for one person to survey a wood on his/her own but there are advantages in using a pair of surveyors. Either a given wood can be split into halves or the surveyors can work together but concentrate on different aspects. For some types of survey two people may be essential. Whilst pairs of surveyors can rarely work as fast as two independent surveyors, the quality of the product is often higher, the morale of the surveyors is usually better, there may be savings on transport costs, and, most importantly, it is much safer. Where surveyors are working more or less separately, clear arrangements should be made for where and when they should check in.

Equipment

Some types of survey require specialist equipment, and in upland areas the standard outdoor survival equipment should be provided. For simple Level 2 surveys of lowland woods the following will probably be needed:

Clipboard (preferably fold-over type)
Ample supply of pens/pencils
Ample supply of recording forms (or notebooks)
Quadrat and quadrat forms
Site maps, preferably 1:10,000 scale, which can be annotated in the field,
  plus clean copies for the write-up
Polythene bags and ties for samples
Compass
Small trowel for soil examination
Protective clothing
Polythene bag to protect recording forms in wet weather
Camera, with spare film
Some form of "identification" and letter giving access permission if appropriate
Lunch

Writing-up

At the outset surveyors should be told how their results will be treated, what sort of report will be prepared, and whether their field records will be stored as they stand or be rewritten in clearer form. Surveyors should be encouraged to make their field notes legible and intelligible without the need to rewrite the forms later. Record forms should be completely filled in, preferably immediately after a site has been visited; otherwise the site may become confused in the surveyor's mind with the next site seen. If a backlog of partially written-up records develops, it is often worth missing a day's surveying to catch up. Where possible, surveyors should be encouraged to write brief written descriptions summarising their views on a wood to supplement the actual field records. This encourages them to look at sites more critically and may highlight features which may not be immediately obvious in the field record. Even if the survey organiser is responsible for the bulk of the survey report, he/she needs to draw heavily on the surveyors' experiences when describing how the methods worked out in practice and any difficulties encountered which may bias the results.

Feedback to site owners

Sometimes owners ask for a copy of the survey results, but, whether they do or not, it is usually helpful in the long run (as well as being common courtesy) if copies of the survey report or a species list can be supplied to them after the survey.

Appendix 3

Recording forms and instructions

Woodland record forms
Instructions for completing woodland record sheets
Examples of woodland record sheets
Quadrat recording in woodland surveys
Instructions for quadrat recording
Examples of quadrat forms

Woodland record forms

At the NCC's woodland survey methods meeting at Belgrave Square (20.2.80), it was agreed that a standard set of woodland recording forms should be produced, to be used for casual visits to woods and for the "walkabout" component of woodland surveys. The forms which are described here are closely based on those in CST Note 2 (Peterken 1977a), which are themselves derived from earlier forms such as R C Steele's Woodland Record Card. The forms are being revised to take account of species name changes but the broad format will remain the same.

General recording forms

Sheet 1 deals with general information about the site which could apply to almost any habitat. Sheet 2 consists of a table of tree and shrub species, with columns for recording their structural type and space for describing other aspects of the structure and management of the wood. Sheet 3 is a vascular plant list restricted to those species associated with woodland. Sheet 4 deals with other habitats (dead wood, glades, etc) within the wood and also has space for notes on other groups of plants and animals or for expanding previous sections. A competent surveyor with a notebook can make as good a record without the need for such complicated-looking forms, but experience suggests that more complete records are obtained (particularly from less experienced surveyors) where there are sections to be filled in or "key words" to jog the memory. It is also quicker to cross off a species name or to tick a structural type box than to write the information out in full. It is impossible to cater for all possibilities with a presence/absence tick-the-box approach and so there is space in all sections for descriptive notes. There is no penalty for continuing these into the next section's space or on to a separate sheet if necessary. For convenience the forms have been produced as two double-sided A4 cards which can be jointed by a hinge of sellotape to form a "leaflet" for each site.

The forms are designed to be used with a full "walkabout" survey. This involves walking through the whole wood either in a series of traverses (say 50-100 m apart) or on a more irregular path to fit the conditions of that wood. Features such as rides or streams encountered en route need to be investigated, but the bulk of the wood must also be adequately covered - not just the easy or exciting bits!

Where quadrats are also to be recorded, the time available for the walkabout component of the survey may be more limited. In some cases the walkabout record is restricted to what is seen on the direct route between the quadrats. The forms should still be used, although clearly this part of the record is less complete than if a full walkabout survey is carried out. Separate forms and instruction sheets for quadrat recording are available. An incomplete record also results where the forms are used by someone making a casual visit to a wood. Such partial records are still useful provided that they are recognised as such and supplemented by future visits. Hence it is important to note to which areas of the wood the record refers and the approximate intensity of survey within these, for example the route followed and the time taken.

In large or complex woods there are advantages in having separate species lists and structural records for different sub-sites, and so separate sheets 2 and 3 (less often 1 and 4) should be completed for each sub-site. When the record produced is a composite one for the whole wood internal variations should be indicated in the notes or (for species) by recording in separate columns. As a rule any site of more than 30 ha is likely to require several records, as are sites with very distinct woodland types within the wood or any site where the surveyor finds himself or herself writing very many notes to describe the internal variation. There is seldom a need to consider areas of less than 1 ha for separate sub-site records unless they are very distinct. Do not combine the results from two woods on one set of forms.

Instructions for completing woodland record sheets 1-4

Complete all sections in black ink so that they can be easily photocopied. Small neat writing makes it easier to fit things in. Some people find it easier to use pencil in the field and ink over it later. Put NI in any section for which you have no information. This helps to pick out where further work is needed.

Sheet 1 - General information

Some of this information can be completed either before or after the field visit, while other sections summarise information which is given in more detail on other sheets.

Region   -   NCC region.
County/region   -)   local authority areas.
District   -)

Record No. - This space is for a filing or archival number. It should be left blank by surveyors.

Owner/tenant/agent - Unless specifically told otherwise, surveyors are themselves responsible for obtaining permission to enter a wood. If permission is obtained from someone other than the owner, record this as it makes it easier for future visits.

Nature Conservation Status - SSSI, NNR, local reserve, etc.

Special interest - Anything for which the wood is already known to be important or which the surveyor comes across and believes to be of particular interest. In the latter case anything written in this section should be expanded elsewhere. For SSSIs the main features from the citation might be included.

Present use/management - A brief summary, e.g. "Pheasant cover, odd tree cut for firewood", "sheep grazing", "timber production". This should be described in more detail on sheet 2.

Other records/old maps, etc. - Refer to any files/reports on the wood. If the wood occurs on old maps give details. Indicate if aerial photographic cover is available or if there are also quadrat records.

Site - Site name, preferably one that is clearly identifiable on a 1:50,000 or 1:25,000 map. Beware of inventing names.

Grid reference - Six-figure grid reference for centre of site, plus letters (or numbers) to identify the 10 km square.

Recorder - Your name is better than just initials.

Map No. - O.S. 1:50,000 (1¼" to 1 mile) sheet number.

Area - In hectares. Ensure that it is clear to what area this refers. Are non-woodland areas within the site boundary or areas of conifer plantations included? Do not estimate the area, as this may lead to subsequent confusion. If necessary, leave it to be measured accurately later.

Date - If more than one visit is made, record all dates.

Map - Where possible attach a copy of a 1:10,000 (6" to 1 mile) map. Alternatively draw a clear sketch map including grid lines so that it is apparent which areas have been visited. Mark on the map any areas not properly visited, variations in vegetation or management, the position of any quadrats, features such as streams or cliffs, approximate location of rare or unusual species, etc. If necessary attach more than one copy of the map so that vegetation type boundaries do not get confused with other features. It is useful to have separate field and fair copies.

Vegetation types - Record the main communities in the wood in terms of a classification system, e.g. Stand Types 4C, 6A, Merlewood (Plot) Types 23, 25, 8, or NVC types. (Increasingly the last will be used in the NCC.) The extent and distribution of at least the main types, however defined, should be marked on the map.

Adjacent land - Tick the appropriate box(es), and add any comments/extra categories in the space provided. More detailed comments may be included on sheet 4, in particular the nature of any transition zones to adjacent semi-natural vegetation. The extent of particular adjacent land-uses may be indicated on the map.

Situation - "Coastal" is within a few miles of the sea. Tick the category (or categories) which best fits the site or write in additional categories. Record aspect (or range of aspect), slope (or range of slope) and altitude (or range).

Soil - Examine the top 30 cm of soil in a few "typical" areas. From a woodland survey viewpoint, the most important characteristics are the following.

(a)   Texture - Which of the three basic soil particles predominates (sand, silt, clay); are stones present; does rock predominate (e.g. boulder field)?

(b)   pH (base-status) - acid (topsoil pH less than 5 approx.), neutral (pH 5-7 approx.), basic (pH more than 7). At the risk of circular arguments, pH can be inferred from ground flora composition.

(c)   Organic matter - Is peat present; what type of humus (mull, moder, mor)?

(d)   Profile drainage - Freely drained, poorly drained, waterlogged (very poorly drained).

(e)   Soil type - Some of the commonest "types" of woodland soil are listed (brown soil, podsol, ranker, rendzina) but there are many others. Alluvium refers to the parent material rather than the type of soil as such. Gley refers to the conditions induced by poor drainage.

Tick any appropriate boxes. Add any comments. If soil maps are available for the area, enter the soil type recorded on these. Soil conditions are usually examined in conjunction with quadrat recording.

Geology - Consult geological maps.

Sheet 2 - Woodland trees and shrubs

Because this part of the recording form may be used separately from the other sheets certain basic information (site name etc) should be recorded on this (as also on sheets 3 and 4).

On the left is a list of woody species with beside them columns of boxes corresponding to different structural forms, though not all may apply to a given species. For convenience some of the smaller species which are unlikely to reach tree size have been grouped at the bottom. (Oak as a climber (Sc) is rare in Britain.) The main structural categories are: T = Trees; C = Coppice; P = Pollards; S = Shrubs (or species contributing to shrub layer, other than coppice); J = Juveniles. These are further subdivided as shown below.

For each species tick the appropriate structural type boxes and estimate abundance on the DAFOR scale (D = dominant; A = abundant; etc) for each box. (Abundance estimates may be done at the end of the visit.)

T   Trees.

Usually single-stemmed individuals (though Tc may be multi-stemmed) in or close below the canopy, usually 5 m or more high.

Ts   Standard trees in a coppice-with-standards (c-w-s) system.
Tn   Self-sown trees. In a c-w-s wood this category is restricted to trees that are contemporary with the existing coppice growth (larger trees = Ts, smaller trees = St).
Tc   Trees which have been promoted from coppice by singling or neglect.
Tp   Trees which have obviously been planted.
Tx   Any other trees which cannot be assigned to one or other of the above categories.

Combinations are possible. Thus Tsp is a standard which was undoubtedly planted.

C   Coppice.

Cx   Coppice cut either close to or at ground level.
Ct   Coppice growth from the cut stump of a tree (hence differing from St or Tn, which are grown from seed but which may be of similar height).

P   Pollards.

Pc   Low pollards (or very high-cut coppice!) cut at 1-2.5 m from the ground.
Px   All other pollards.

S   Shrubs (usually 0.5-5 m high).

Sx   Shrubs, which may be either small (= Ss), judged on height and spread, or large (= Sl).
Sc   Climber.
St   Maiden stem of tree species larger than a sapling, but not yet a tree; in a coppice wood post-dating the coppice. Its presence in the shrub layer is only temporary, as it grows through.

J   Juveniles.

Js   Seedings (usually less than 25 cm). In a grazed wood "seedlings" may be several years old, but repeatedly browsed back to less than 25 cm tall.
Jp   Sapling)
) up to 2 m high for some tree species.
Jv   Suckers)

Ancient Semi-natural, etc. - "Ancient" sites are those which have a continuous history of woodland going back at least to 1600. In the absence of other information, the presence of a wood on a First Edition O.S. map is an indication that it may be ancient. "Semi-natural" means that most of the trees appear to have originated by natural regeneration or are long-established stools. "Plantations" are where most individuals have obviously been planted. These distinctions cannot always be made in the field. Indicate which combinations (there may be more than one) are present on the site by marking the appropriate box(es). Record either on the map or in the notes made on this sheet the approximate extent of each combination.

Space for notes - Describe the variations within the wood in the species composition of the tree and shrub layers and in the ground flora communities. A standardised procedure for doing this (Table 18), developed in Scotland, is as follows.

Canopy layer - abundance, height and diameter of each species and cover for the whole layer; shrub layer - abundance and height of each species and cover for the whole layer; ground flora - abundance of the commoner species. The boundaries of the canopy and ground flora variations may or may not coincide. Where possible, these variations should be assigned to the appropriate vegetation type in the field.

Describe the management and use of the wood (both past and present), the nature of any boundaries (walls, ditches, fences, banks, etc), either internal or external. Note any signs of grazing and its intensity.

Area occupied by each type - Assign the types or communities recognised in the notes above (using whatever system of classification) to approximate "area" categories, based on your assessment of roughly what percentage of the wood is occupied by each and a knowledge of the total area of the wood. Alternatively leave this space blank if the areas are to be accurately measured from your map later.

Tree Layer - Record an approximate mean height for the trees on site (or a range if this is very variable). Record an estimate of percentage cover for the tree layer. (It helps to stop from time to time and make a note of these at particular points. The figures can then be combined to give an overall value.)

Shrub Layer - Repeat for the shrub layer.

Age class abundance (all species) - Assess on the DAFOR scale the abundance of the different age classes of trees and of coppice. Over-mature trees and saplings are the age classes most frequently missing from British woods and are perhaps the most important. Over-mature trees are "good" for invertebrates and epiphytes; saplings indicate successful regeneration. Determining the age of a tree from its appearance is very subjective, but some approximate guidelines are given below.

Over-mature trees - More than about 75 cm diameter breast height (dbh) for large species such as oak, beech and sycamore; about 50 cm for birch and pine.

Mature trees - More than about 20 cm dbh and more than about 8 m tall; these usually form the bulk of the canopy.

Young trees - More than about 5 cm dbh or about 2 m high, found in shrub layer or lower canopy; these may form patches in which they are the canopy. (Note that this includes rather more than just the St category included in the structural categories.)

Saplings/suckers - Regeneration between about 25 cm and 2 m high, less than 5 cm dhb, of several years' growth.

Seedlings - Regeneration less than 25 cm, including stems of several years' growth kept short by browsing.

Coppice - Enter abundance where it exists as a distinct layer under a canopy.

Sheet 3 - Woodland vascular plants

Time on site - The number of species found is affected by the intensity of searching, which in turn depends on the time spent searching. Record the time spent on this part of the survey.

Species list - This list is of "woodland species" only, i.e. shade-bearers, shade-casters and edge species. There are probably some omissions. "Non-woodland" species also occur in woods and these extra species and any short comments on the distribution of species can be recorded in the space provided. In some woods there are large open areas within the wood which are essentially non-woodland habitats (grassland, bog, heath). As a rule surveyors should concentrate on producing a complete species list for the woodland component of the site only and regard other habitats as subsidiary from the point of view of assessing the site as woodland.

Species' names should be scored through when they are seen and an estimate of abundance (DAFOR scale) put in the column, usually at the end of a visit. Two columns are provided so that a distinction can be made between different parts of the wood or between old and new records. The two boxes at the bottom of the sheet (Woodland species No., Total species No.) are for use in evaluation. They do not need to be completed in the field.

Species names up till now have followed Clapham, Tutin & Warburg (CTW) (1962), except for ferns, which follow the revised names given in the atlas of ferns (Jermy et al. 1978). Changes in fern names relative to CTW are given below.

CTW	Fern atlas	English name
Dryopteris borreri	Dryopteris pseudomas	Scaly male-fern
D. dilata	D. austriaca	Broad buckler fern
Phyllitis scolopendrium	Asplenium scolopendrium	Hart's-tongue
Thelypteris dryopteris	Gymnocarpium dryopteris	Oak fern
T. robertiana	G. robertianum	Limestone fern
T. limbosperma	Oreopteris limbosperma	Lemon-scented fern
(T. oreopteris)		
T. palustris	Thelypteris thelypteroides	Marsh fern
T. phegopteris	Phegopteris connectilis	Beech fern

A full revised list based on the third edition of Excursion flora (Clapham, Tutin & Warburg 1983) will be introduced shortly.

Sheet 4 - Habitats, vegetation-structure, other groups

Ideally the record for a wood should include lists for other groups of plants and animals. This is impracticable. However, certain habitat features or types of vegetation structure can be used as "indicators" for these groups.

Other comments - This is a space for continuing the description from sheet 2 and for summarising general impressions of the site.

Habitats in or close to wood - The major classes of habitat are listed, with "key-words" to jog the memory. Enter "P" or "N" in the box beside each. Since no survey is complete, it is impossible to say that a particular habitat is absent, only that it was either present (P) or not seen (N). If the habitat is present, write brief descriptive notes.

A pond 2 m across in a 100 ha wood has less of an impact on that site as a whole than three ponds 20 m across in a 30 ha wood. Therefore surveyors are requested to enter "S" in the box by a habitat if they feel that in this wood it is particularly important. This is highly subjective and will vary from surveyor to surveyor, but it should nevertheless help to pick out the extreme cases. If "S" is entered, it must be supported by a fairly detailed decription of the habitat or feature concerned.

Vegetation structure - The same applies as for "habitats". The herb, shrub and tree layers will already have been recorded in some detail on sheets 2 and 3. There is no need to repeat what is already recorded, but more general statements about them may be made here. Since epiphytes and bryophytes are unlikely to be recorded in detail, any general descriptive notes on these may be useful.

Other groups - The records made in this section depend on the time available and the knowledge of the surveyor. A list of common/important bryophytes and lichens is included with the instructions for quadrat recording. Although very subjective, it is worth recording that the wood seemed to have "lots of butterflies" or to be "noisy with bird song" or to have "a good display of fungi". It does at least show that these groups are present, whereas no conclusions can be drawn from a complete absence of any record. Similarly, records of common species such as squirrels, deer or blackbirds are a start towards more detailed work.

WOODLAND RECORD SHEET 1

South Region	Buckinghamshire	District		Record No.
Region	County			

OWNER/tenant/agent The Claydon Estate	None Nature Conservation Status	SITE Shrubs Wood	
	Good semi-natural structure	SP699245 GRID REF.	K. Kirby RECORDER
Permission to enter from Estate Office	Special Interest None apparent	Vegetation types Ash-maple coppice (2A)	1:50,000 O.S. sheet 165 Map No.
	Present use/management		Area 7.5 ha
	Regional files. 19th C. maps show the site with much the same Other records/old maps, etc. boundary.		26.5.81 DATE

MAP

Farm worker commented that "there used to be butterfly orchids in the rides before they got so overgrown".

ADJACENT LAND

Intensively farmed land, part arable, part improved pasture.

Broadleaf wood		Mixed wood	
Conifer wood		Scrub	
Lowland grass		Parkland	
Lowland heath		Orchard	
Upland grass		Arable/ley	/
Upland heath		Garden	
Bog/peatland		Fen	
Moving water		Still water	
Buildings	/	Road/railway	

SITUATION

Valley side		Hill slope	
Valley bottom		Hill top	
Plain	/	Coastal	
Plateau		Inland	/

Aspect —

Slope —

Altitude 325 - 350 feet

SOIL Very wet after recent rain. Mostly neutral-basic clay.

Sand		Stones	
Silt		Rock	
Clay	/	Peat	
Acid		Mull	/
Neutral	/	Moder	
Basic	/	Mor	
Podsol		Water-logged	/
Brown soil	/		
Rendzina		Poorly-drained	/
Ranker			
Alluvium		Freely-drained	
Gley	/		

GEOLOGY

LAT 51° 55'

MIDDLE CLAYDON PH

Shrubs Wood

- - - route taken

① etc. notes, see overleaf.

═ overgrown ride

deep boundary ditches

WOODLAND TREES AND SHRUBS · 2

	Tx	Tp	Ts	Tc	Tn	Cx	Ct	Px	Pc	Sx	Sc	St	Js	Jp	Jv
Acer cam					F										
Acer pse															
Aescu hip															
Alnus glu															
Betul pend					O										
Betul pub															
Carp bet															
Casta sat															
Conifer sp															
Coryl ave						F									
Crata mon										O					
Crata oxy										F					
Euony eur															
Fagus syl															
Frang aln															
Fraxi exc			O	F									O		
Ilex aqu															
Junip com															
Larix sp															
Malus syl										O					
Picea sp															
Pinus syl															
Popul tre				O											O
Prunu avi															
Prunu lau															
Prunu pad															
Prunu spi										F					O
Querc cer															
Querc pet															
Querc rob			F	R											
Rhamn cat															
Rhodo pon															
Salix alb															
Salix aur															
Salix cap				O											
Salix cin															
Salix fra															
Salix pen															
Salix vim															
Sambu nig										O			R		
Sorbu ari															
Sorbu auc															
Sorbu tor															
Taxus bac															
Thely san										O					
Tilia cor															
Tilia eur															
Tilia pla															
Ulmus car															
Ulmus gla															
Ulmus pro															
Vibur lan															

	Tx	Tp	Ts	Tc	Tn	Cx	Ct	Px	Pc	Sx	Sc	St	Js	Jp	Jv
	Sx	Sc		Js	Jp	Jv					Sx	Sc	Js	Jp	Jv
Clem vit								Ribes syl							
Daph lau								Ribes uva							
Heder hel								Rosa arv							
Ligus vul	R							Rosa can							
Lonic per		F						Sarot sco							
Mahon aqu								Ulex eur							
Myrica ga								Ulex gal							
Ribes nig								Vibur opu	R						

County **Buckinghamshire**

Recorder **K. Kirby**

SITE **Shrubs Wood**

Date **26.5.81**   GRID REF. **SP 699 245**

Ancient Semi-nat.	Recent Semi-nat.	Ancient plantn.	Recent plantn.
✓			

D = dominant · A = abundant · F = frequent · O = occasional · R = rare

Stand description · Management and use · History · Nature of boundaries · Grazing

① Oak standards → 80cm dbh, occasional singled oak, ash coppice poles + hazel, field maple, thorn understorey. Blackthorn thickets Ground flora End. n.s., Galeob. lut., Milium eff., Des. cesp., Mercurialis. Very wet, shallow channels in soil surface. **2A**

Wet, rather overgrown ride with tall grasses and sedges.

② Ash more common in the canopy. Understorey of hazel, hawthorn and blackthorn. Des. cesp. locally abundant, with Glech. hed., Circaea lut., Valeriana off., Poa triv.. Dryer areas with much Endymion n.s. **2A**

Old canopy gaps invaded by patches of birch and field maple

③ Neglected ash-field maple coppice, few standards Understorey probably last cut c1950. Ground flora: Mercurialis, Galeob. lut., Urtica dioica Endymion n.s. **2A**

④ Scattered oak and field maple standards → 50cm dbh. Ash, birch, aspen poles over hazel, hawthorn understorey with dense Lonicera tangles. Ground flora: Endymion n.s., Galeob. lut, Stellaria holostea, Glechoma hed., Circaea lut.

⑤ Tree and shrub layer similar to ④ but occasional ash standard. Ground flora dominated by dog's mercury and nettles. **2A**

⑥ Tree and shrub layer as ④. Ground flora: Milium effusum, Endymion non-scriptus, Des. cesp. Scrophularia nodosa, Galeob. lut., Circaea lut.,

Area occupied by each type

0 – 0.5 ha	0.5 – 2	2 – 10	10 – 20	20 + ha
		2A		

	Height	Cover		Height	Cover
Tree Layer	10–12 m	90%	Shrub Layer	2–3 m	40%

Age class abundance (all species)

O/mature (oak)	mature oak-ash	young trees various	saplings	seedlings	coppice mainly hazel
R	A	F	R	O	F

Tp Planted tree · Cx coppice · Sc climber
Tn Self-sown tree · Ct regrowth from stump · St young tree
Ts standard in c-w-s · Px pollard (2.5m+) · Js seedling
Tc grown from coppice · Pc pollard (1–2.5m) · Jp sapling
Tx any other tree · Sx shrub · Jv sucker

WOODLAND VASCULAR PLANTS 3

Species	Abundance
~~Acer camp~~	F
–Acer plat	
–Acer pseu	
3Acon angl	
1Actaea sp	
Adoxa mos	
–Aegop pod	
–Aesc hipp	
Agrop can	
Agros can	
Agros gig	
Agros sto	
Agros ten	
~~Ajuga rep~~	F
Alch glab	
Alch vest	
Alch xant	
Allia pet	
All ursin	
Alnus glu	
~~Anem nem~~	R
~~Angel syl~~	R
Anthox od	
~~Anthr syl~~	R
Aquil vul	
Arct lapp	
Arct min	
Arrh elat	
2Arum ital	
~~Arum mac~~	[illegible]
1Asarum eu	
Aspl adia	
Aspl scol	
Aspl tric	
Aspl viri	
Athyr f-f	
Atropa be	
Beton off	
~~Bet pendu~~	O
Bet pubes	
Blech spi	
~~Brach syl~~	O
Bryon dio	
1Buxus sem	
Calam can	
Calam epi	
Calluna v	
Calth pal	
Calyst se	
Camp lat	
1Camp patu	
Camp rot	
Camp trac	
Card acan	
Card amar	
~~Card flex~~	R
2Card impa	
Card prat	
Car acuti	
Car biner	
3Car capil	
3Car diand	
1Car digit	
1Car elong	
Car hirta	
Car laevi	
Car monta	
Car palle	
Car panic	
Car pendu	
Car pseud	
~~Car remot~~	O
Car ripar	
Car strig	
~~Car sylva~~	O
Carpi bet	
–Cast sati	
Ceph dama	
1Ceph long	
Cham ang	
Chrys alt	
Chrys opp	
Circ alpi	
Circ inte	
~~Circ lute~~	F
Cirs hete	
~~Cirs palu~~	R

Species	Abundance
Cirs vulg	
Clem vita	
Colch aut	
Con macul	
Conop maj	
Conva maj	
1Coral tri	
Coryd cla	
~~Coryl ave~~	F
~~Crat mono~~	O
~~Crat oxya~~	F
Crep palu	
Cyst frag	
Dact fuch	
Dact glom	
Daph laur	
1Daph meze	
1Dent bulb	
~~Desch cae~~	A
Desch fle	
Digit pur	
Dips pilo	
Dryop aem	
~~Dry aust~~	O
Dry cart	
~~Dry f-mas~~	O
Dry psmas	
~~Endym non~~	A
–Epil aden	
Epil hirs	
~~Epil mont~~	R
Epil obsc	
Epil rose	
Epil tetr	
1Epip atro	
Epip hell	
1Epip lep	
Epip phyl	
Epip purp	
Equis hye	
Equis pal	
Equis syl	
Equis tel	
–Eranth hy	
Euon euro	
Eupat can	
Euph amyg	
Euph lath	
Fagus syl	
2Festu alt	
~~Festu gig~~	O
Fest ovin	
Fest rubr	
~~Filip ulm~~	O
Frag vesc	
~~Fran exce~~	F
Frang aln	
3Gagea lut	
Galan niv	
~~Galeob lu~~	F
Galeo tet	
~~Gal apari~~	F
Gal odora	
~~Gal palus~~	R
Gal saxat	
Geran luc	
Geran rob	
Geran san	
Geran syl	
Geum riva	
Geum urba	
~~Glech hed~~	A
Gnaph syl	
3Goody rep	
Gymn dryo	
3Gymn robe	
Hedera he	
2Hell foet	
Hell viri	
Herac sph	
Hierac sp	
~~Holc lana~~	O
Holc moll	
2Hord euro	

Species	Abundance
Humul Lup	
Hym tunbr	
Hym wilso	
Hyper and	
Hyper hir	
Hyper hum	
Hyper mac	
3Hyper mon	
Hyper per	
Hyper pul	
Hyper tet	
Ilex aqui	
1Impat nol	
–Impat par	
Inul cony	
Iris foet	
Iris pseu	
Junc acut	
Junc cong	
Junc effu	
Junip com	
Lam album	
Laps comm	
Lathr squ	
Lath mont	
Lath sylv	
Ligus vul	
1Lili mart	
1Linn bore	
List cord	
List ovat	
~~Lonic per~~	F
Luz forst	
–Luz luzul	
Luz multi	
Luz pilos	
Luz sylva	
~~Lych flos~~	O
Lycop eur	
Lys nemor	
Lys vulga	
Lyth sali	
~~Malus syl~~	O
2Mecan cam	
1Melam cri	
Melam pra	
1Melam syl	
Melic nut	
Melic uni	
2Mel melis	
Menth aqu	
Menth arv	
~~Merc pere~~	A
~~Mil effus~~	F
Moehr tri	
Molin cae	
Mones uni	
Mono h.pi	
–Mont sibi	
Mycel mur	
Myos arve	
Myos sylv	
Myo aquat	
Myri gale	
Narc pseu	
Neot nidu	
Ophr apif	
Ophr inse	
Orch masc	
Oreop lim	
1Orch purp	
1Orni pyre	
3Oroba hed	
2Orth secu	
Osmun reg	
Oxal acet	
Paris qua	
Petas hyb	
Pheg con	
Pimp majo	
Pinus syl	
Plat bifo	
Plat chlo	

Species	Abundance
Poa annua	
Poa chaix	
Poa nemor	
~~Poa trivi~~	F
Polyg mul	
1Polyg odo	
Poly dume	
Polyp int	
Polyp vul	
Polys acu	
Polys set	
Pop canes	
Pop nigra	
~~Pop tremu~~	O
Pot angli	
Pot anser	
Pot erect	
Pot repta	
Pot steri	
1Prim elat	
Prim veri	
~~Prim vulg~~	O
Prun vulg	
Pru avium	
–Pru lauro	
Pru padus	
~~Pru spino~~	F
Pter aqui	
1Pulm long	
–Pulm offi	
2Pyrol med	
Pyrol min	
2Pyrol rot	
Pyrus com	
–Querc cer	
Querc pet	
~~Querc rob~~	F
Ran auric	
Ran ficar	
Ran flamm	
~~Ran repen~~	O
Rham cath	
–Rhod pont	
1Ribes alp	
Ribes nig	
1Ribes spi	
Ribes syl	
Ribes uva	
Rosa arve	
Rosa cani	
Rosa duma	
Rosa micr	
Rosa obtu	
Rosa rubi	
Rosa sher	
Rosa styl	
Rosa tome	
Rosa vill	
Rubia per	
Rubu caes	
~~Rubu frut~~	O
Rubu idea	
Rubu saxa	
Rum acosa	
Rum aclla	
Rum congl	
Rum obtus	
Rum sangu	
Rusc acul	
Salix alb	
Salix aur	
~~Salix cap~~	O
Salix cin	
Salix fra	
Salix pen	
Salix pur	
Salix tri	
Salix vim	
~~Samb nigr~~	O
Sanic eur	
Sapon off	
Saro scop	
Scirp syl	
Scro aqua	
~~Scro nodo~~	O
2Scro umbr	

Species	Abundance
Sedum for	
Sedum tel	
Senec syl	
2Sibth eur	
~~Silen dio~~	F
~~Solan dul~~	O
Solid vir	
Sorb aria	
Sorb aucu	
1Sorb devo	
1Sorb porr	
3Sorb rupi	
Sorb torm	
Stach pal	
~~Stach syl~~	O
Stel alsi	
Stel gram	
~~Stel holo~~	F
~~Stel medi~~	R
Stel negl	
Stel nemo	
Succ prat	
Tamus com	
Tarax off	
Taxus bac	
Teuc scor	
Thali min	
~~Thel sang~~	O
3Thely the	
Tilia cor	
Tilia eur	
1Tilia pla	
Toril jap	
Trien eur	
Troll eur	
Ulex euro	
Ulmus car	
Ulmus gla	
Ulmus pro	
~~Urtic dio~~	O
Vacc myrt	
Vacc viti	
Valer dio	
~~Valer off~~	R
~~Veron cha~~	O
Veron hed	
Veron mon	
Veron off	
Vib lanta	
~~Vib opulu~~	R
1Vicia byt	
3Vicia oro	
~~Vicia sep~~	R
Vicia syl	
Vinca min	
Viola arv	
Viola hir	
Viola odo	
Viola pal	
Viola rei	
~~Viola riv~~	R
Wahl hede	
1Zerna ben	
~~Zerna ram~~	O
Rumex sp.	O
Rosa sp.	R

COUNTY Buckinghamshire

SITE Shrubs Wood

GRID REF.	DATE
SP699245	26.5.81

RECORDER	TIME ON SITE
K. Kirby	1hr

Ride flora not properly recorded but includes
Lathyrus pratensis
Lotus uliginosus
Carex riparia
Dactylis glomerata

WOODLAND SPECIES No.

TOTAL SPECIES No.

– Introductions to G.B.
3 only in 60–100, 10km squares
2 „ „ 30–60, „ „
1 „ „ 16–30, „ „

D = dominant, A = abundant, F = frequent, O = Occasional, R = Rare

Recorder	Date	Grid Ref.	Site

Other comments: Ride could be improved for conservation if it was opened up.

HABITATS IN OR CLOSE TO WOOD		
RIDES, GLADES, OPEN AREAS vegetation-size-shade-permanence-edges	P	Ride narrow (c 4m) and now shaded. Wet tall grass, herb, sedge community. Otherwise no real clearings. Some past gaps in the canopy now filled by birch.
PONDS, STREAMS, RIVERS vegetation-size-substrate-type of bank-shade-permanence-speed of flow	P	Numerous small depressions and shallow surface channels which act as temporary streams and pools after rain. Ditches round the edge of the wood have been recently deepened.
ROCKS Size-abundance-outcrop-scree-cliff-gorges-surface stone-acid-basic	N	
BOG, FEN, FLUSHES vegetation-size-wetness-acid-basic-organic-inorganic	N	
DEAD WOOD Size-felled or fallen-abundance-decay-logs-branches-standing trees-holes or hollows	P	Some dead standing birches, plus dead lower limbs on former oak standards
OTHER HABITATS OR COMMUNITIES including adjacent land-transitions-nearest woodland		Shrubs Wood is part of a group of woods on the estate which shows a transition from oak-hazel communities to oak-ash-field maple types, the latter being the more species-rich (and includes Shrubs Wood). Decoy Pond Wood and Sheephouse are only a field away.
VEGETATION STRUCTURE		Little bare ground but much litter where the understorey is
BARE GROUND extent-distribution-sunny banks	P	dense. Bryophytes not recorded but appear to be sparse both
LITTER LAYER: drifts, thickness, type of litter	P	on the ground and small dead lying branches. Ground
BRYOPHYTE LAYER – on wood-on rocks-on ground- carpets	P	flora mainly dominated by low herbs such as Mercurialis and Endymion but grasses such as Deschampsia and
HERB LAYER – height-cover-distribution-broad type	P	Milium are locally abundant.
SHRUB LAYER – height-cover-uniformity	P	Dense shrub layer through most of the wood, c 30yrs old hazel, field maple, former coppice plus shrubs such as
TREE LAYER – height-cover-uniformity-age		hawthorn and blackthorn. Mature to over-mature oak standards (plus a few ash and field maple) 60-80 cm dbh
EPIPHYTES/CREEPERS – type-position on tree-abundance		perhaps 80-100yrs old plus outgrown coppice poles of
OTHER GROUPS	NI	ash (c 30-50 yrs). Birch patches are about the same
BRYOPHYTES & LICHENS	NI	age as the ash so may have invaded when the ash was
VERTEBRATES	NI	last cut.
INVERTEBRATES	NI	
FUNGI	NI	
Record species seen or signs of their presence, plus any features that indicate the value of the wood for these groups.		

P = Present, N = Not seen, S = Significant feature

Quadrat recording in woodland surveys

In 1980 it was agreed that future quadrat records should as far as possible be compatible with the requirements of the three classification systems which were available then or which would be available shortly. The NCC will adopt the National Vegetation Classification for most purposes in the future, but it is useful to be able to fit any records into the Stand Type or Merlewood (Plot Type) classifications also. These classifications are still being used and there are many past records which have been made according to these systems.

The Merlewood 14.1 x 14.1 m (200 m²) plot was taken as the basic unit. It is recorded as a series of nested plots (see Figure 30) so that the results for a 5 x 5 or 10 x 10 m plot can be extracted for use with the NVC. 200 m² is, however, too small an area to provide an adequate record for the tree and shrub layers. Therefore it was proposed to record any additional tree and shrub species in a further 10 m fringe. This means that the tree and shrub layers are considered over an area roughly 34 m x 34 m, i.e. big enough to classify the record using the Stand Type system. The differences between the record for 34 x 34 m and that for 50 x 50 m, as used in the NVC, are likely to be small.

For surveys using Stand Types or Plot Types, this kind of quadrat should continue to be used. It will also be useful where it is necessary to have records for the tree and shrub layers over the same area as for the ground flora record. For surveys where the main (or only) use for quadrat data is to classify the stands according to the National Vegetation Classification, the simpler NVC style of quadrat recording may be followed. An example of an NVC form is given on p. 132. The various boxes should be self-explanatory; they are similar to those used in the Merlewood system.

The way the quadrats are positioned in the wood is determined by the purposes of the survey and is discussed in the main text. Note that the NVC approach (and to a lesser extent the Stand Type system) assumes that the plot is placed in a more or less homogeneous area. If, for other reasons, random, stratified random or systematic plot distributions are to be used, it may be better to use the nested quadrat.

"Real" or "imaginary" quadrats

NVC quadrats are marked out by pacing: no poles or strings are required. A "real" quadrat delineated by strings and poles (Figure 30) is used for the 200 m² plot in the Bunce & Shaw (1973) method. This is necessary if the plot is to be recorded as a series of nested quadrats and ensures a more thorough searching of the area. The original quadrat poles used by Bunce & Shaw are cumbersome and so a "miniaturised" version is described. This is adequate for most occasions, although some problems may occur in very tall vegetation. The outer 10 m fringe used in recording the tree and shrub layers can be estimated by eye and pacing. Its precise outer boundary ($\pm$ 3 m) is not important.

Photographs

Film is relatively cheap compared to other survey costs, so surveyors should be encouraged to take photographs of the sites. The better documented these are, the better. Note the location and date as the minimum, but preferably also the direction of the shot and the main feature it is meant to show (as this may not be obvious). The inclusion of features or people for scale is helpful.

Figure 30   Diagram of a "real" quadrat

The bulk of the records concern the 200 m² plot only. The records for the tree and shrub layers and the plot description must also take account of a surrounding 10 m strip (approximately).

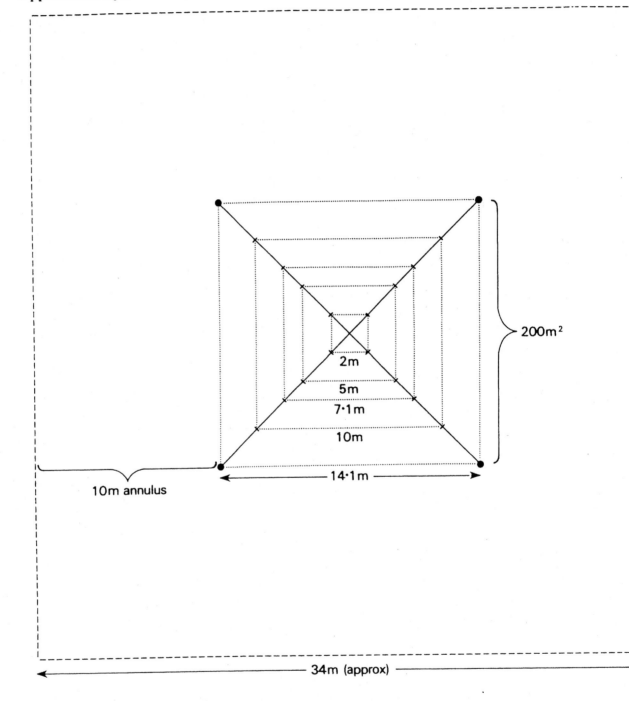

● =   quadrat poles connected by strings, forming diagonals to the 200 m² plot (14.1 m x 14.1 m). Markers along the string indicate the corners of the smaller quadrats as follows:

2 x 2 m (4 m²)	– markers	1.42 m from centre
5 x 5 m (25 m²)	– markers	3.54 m from centre
7.1 x 7.1 m (50 m²)	– markers	5.00 m from centre
10 x 10 m (100 m²)	– markers	7.07 m from centre
14.1 x 14.1 m (200 m²)	– markers	10.00 m from centre

Instructions for quadrat recording based on a 200 m² quadrat (Bunce & Shaw 1973)

Locate the plot position. This will either be predetermined before you enter the wood or you will be told to allocate positions according to the variation which is present in the wood.

Set up the plot. Surveyors may be told how the plot is to be orientated, e.g. always with one diagonal running N-S. In practice 75% of the plot area is the same whatever the orientation.

Complete record sheets 1 and 2 for the plot.

Sheet 1 - Ground flora

(a)   Complete the top line (Date, Recorder, etc).

(b)   Record the vascular plants present in the innermost 4 m² quadrat in the appropriate section on the form. (The dotted lines are simply to help keep the names straight.) When this is complete, move out to the next set of marks on the diagonal strings (equivalent to a 25 m² quadrat). Record additional species (those not found in the smaller 4 m² quadrat) in the 25 m² section of the form. Repeat this process for the three larger quadrats, each time recording only species not already found. If a species is borderline between successive quadrat sizes, do not waste time deciding which to put it in: it is unlikely to be critical.

(c)   Record any woody seedlings or small saplings (less than about 100 cm high) along with other vascular plants.

(d)   Record any bryophytes or lichens, as far as you are able, as for vascular plants. Note the substrate (rock, wood, etc) for species not growing on the ground. If you cannot identify bryophytes or lichens you will be given separate instructions as to what to do about collecting samples.

(e)   Estimate the cover for each species over the whole 200 m² plot, using the Domin scale, and record it in the column headed C/A. (Percentage cover values may be used if preferred as long as use is consistent in any one survey.) The other column is for a coding number to be inserted if the results need to be fed into a computer (e.g. for classification).

(f)   At the bottom of the sheet are boxes for the number of vascular plant species, number of bryophytes and number of woody species. These do not need to be completed in the field.

Sheet 2 - Plot description, Tree and shrub record

(a)   Complete details under Date, Recorder, etc in case this sheet gets separated from Sheet 1.

(b)   For the whole 200 m² plot, estimate the percentage cover to the nearest 10% of the following:

Bare soil - exposed soil or small stones/gravel (less than 5 cm across).

Rock - often covered by bryophytes; record only exposed rock here but indicate in notes the extent of bryophyte-covered rock.

Water - ponds, streams, etc; do not record rain even if it is covering 100% of the plot!

Wood - logs, stumps (more than 5 cm across).

Litter - recognisable plant remains, tree leaves, dead grass or bracken fronds.

Bryophytes - include lichens with bryophytes and estimate overall cover. It is important that this record be made even if the individual species are not collected or identified; include in the description an indication of their luxuriance and the substrate on which they are found.

Herb layer - include herbs, grasses, ferns, low woody species such as bramble, and regeneration.

When one is estimating percentage cover for the foregoing categories it is difficult to allow for the overlap of different layers - bare earth beneath plants, for instance. This may mean that the percentages will not add up to 100%. Some surveyors try to avoid this by attempting to estimate coverage only at the uppermost layer over any point. Provided that you are consistent within the survey, either approach is acceptable.

Shrub layer - include all woody individuals from about 50 cm up to about 5 m high whether these are shrubs, coppice or young trees. Some flexibility in defining the upper limit is permissible, if for example there is a discontinuity in the canopy above 6 m. The lower limit includes all woody plants which have not been recorded on sheet 1. Bramble, roses, honeysuckle, ivy, <u>Clematis</u> <u>vitalba</u> etc are usually included with the ground flora.

Tree layer - all woody individuals above the shrub layer and usually forming the canopy. Exceptionally individuals less than 5 m may be included in the "tree layer", for example if the plot is in a young thicket or plantation. This should be made clear in the notes.

Open sky - the tree and shrub layers may overlap but do not necessarily give complete cover. Therefore estimate separately the area of the plot not covered by either. If it is winter, imagine that the leaves are on the trees and then make the estimate.

(c) List tree and shrub species present in the 200 m² plot and enter "P" (= present) in the column head "Present/No". For species contributing to the tree layer (defined above), record in the same column the number of stems within the plot. If there are large numbers of stems, count the number in one quarter of the plot and estimate the total. If most individuals are multi-stemmed (as in former coppice), record the number of <u>stools</u> present and indicate the approximate number of stems per stool. Make sure it is clear whether it is the number of stems or of stools which has been recorded. Note any additional tree and shrub species occurring in the 10 m surround by entering "N" (= not present in 200 m² plot).

(d) The column headed "Regen." may be ignored in the field. Any regeneration of trees and shrubs should already have been recorded with the ground flora. However, it is useful to transfer these records subsequently to this column.

(e) Using the Domin scale, estimate the contribution of each species to the shrub layer cover <u>over the whole area (200 m² + 10 m surround)</u> and record this in the column headed SHRUB. Note that young trees or coppice may contribute to the cover in the shrub layer as defined here. Do the same for the tree layer and record this in the column headed TREE. Again shrubs may contribute to the tree layer in some woods.

(f) Record the mean diameter and/or diameter range for the <u>trees</u> only, in the final column. By convention, diameter measurements are given as diameter breast height (dbh), which is taken as 1.3 m from the ground. Only <u>a rough estimate</u> is required - so do not take more than a couple of minutes on this. This column can also be used for any short comments about the growth form or state of a particular species, e.g. "planted", "maiden", "pollards", "coppice", "sucker" or "trees dying".

(g) Record mean height and/or height range for the tree and shrub layers separately. If there is marked variation, the range is more useful than the mean. Again only an estimate is needed.

(h) Estimate the overall slope of the plot (if any). If the slope varies within the plot to any great extent, record this in the description. Record the aspect of the slope and indicate any variation in aspect within the plot.

(i) Write brief notes on what is in the 200 m² plot and how it relates to the 10 m surround and to other areas of the wood; i.e. does it look very different from any other area of the wood that you have seen or is it fairly typical? There are some key words on the form to jog your memory. These are expanded below.

Stumps	-	size, abundance, state of decay
Logs	-	fallen branches, other dead wood, size, abundance, decay
Dead trees	-	still standing (e.g. after Dutch elm disease), also dead branches on trees or holes in the trunk
Epiphytes	-	moss or lichen on trees, large fungi, creepers (ivy, <u>Clematis</u>, honeysuckle)
Litter	-	depth and type (tree leaves, grass, bracken, etc), any drifts
Rock	-	size and abundance of stones, boulders, outcrops, cliffs or scree
Bare ground	-	particularly dry sandy areas or sunny banks (good for insects)
Pools/Streams	-	size, substrate, speed of flow, nature of banks, whether steam shaded, any associated vegetation
Open areas	-	any glades or knolls, their size and associated vegetation
Vegetation	-	any thickets (roses, bramble, blackthorn, etc), clumps of tall herbs, moss carpets, fern banks, short grass, long grass, heath type
Animals	-	dung, tracks, hair, burrows or other signs
Grazing	-	intensity, species
Management	-	coppice, signs of felling, recreational use, shooting, etc
Walls	-	walls, hedges, tracks, rubbish or other signs of human activity

130

GROUND FLORA   SHEET 1

Date 15-7-82 Recorder K. Kirby Plot no. 2	R.O.M. Edgar	Grid ref. TQ 228358 Site House Copse		

$4m^2$ quadrat. Species	C/A	$25m^2$ Q. (cont.)	C/A
Poa trivialis	4		
Fraxinus excelsior (seedling)	4		
Rubus fruticosus	5		
Endymion non-scriptus	5		
Hedera helix	4		
Crataegus monogyna (seedling)	2		
		$50m^2$Q. Ilex aquifolium (seedling)	1
		Holcus cf. lanatus	2
		$100m^2$Q. Stellaria media	2
		Moehringia trinervia	3
		Quercus robur (seedling)	1
		Mercurialis perennis	1
$25m^2$Q. Digitalis purpurea	1		
		$200m^2$Q. Oxalis acetosella	1

10=91-100, 9=76-90, 8=51-75, 7=34-50, 6=26-33	No. Bryo-phytes		No. Woody species		No. Vasc. plants	
5=11-25, 4=4-10, 3=freq., 2=sparse, 1=rare						

PLOT DESCRIPTION, TREE AND SHRUB RECORD   SHEET 2

Date 15.7.82	Recorder **R.D.M. Edgar** K. Kirby	Plot No. 2		Grid Ref. TQ22835	Site House Copse		

% cover 200m² only	Bare soil	—	Rock	-	Water	—	Wood	<5	Litter	35
	Bryophytes	<5	Herb layer	60	Shrub layer	5	Tree layer	100	Open sky	—

Species	Present/No 200m² only	Regen. 200m² only	Cover (domin) 200m² + 10m² SHRUB	TREE	Diameter, growth form
Crataegus monogyna	P	Js 2	Sx 3		— — — — —
Tilia cordata	P 7 stools			Tc 8	stems 15 - 20 cm
Quercus robur	P 3	Js 1		Ts Tc 6	50 - 70 cm
Ilex aquifolium	P	Js 1	Sx 2		— — — — —
Crataegus oxyacanthoides	N				— — — — —
Carpinus betulus	N			Tc 4	stems 15 cm
Corylus avellana	N		Sx 3		— — — — —
Fraxinus excelsior	P	Js 4			— — — — —

1=rare 2=sparse 3=freq. 4= 4-10 5=11-25 6=26-33 7=34-50 8=51-75 9=76-90 10=91-100	Height range Shrub layer 2-3 M	Height range Tree layer 16 m
	ASPECT —	SLOPE —

Presence in 200m² plot of: Stumps, Logs Dead trees Epiphytes Litter, Rock Bare ground Pools, Streams Open areas Vegetation Animals Grazing Management Walls	DESCRIPTION Small ditch across one corner. Most of the ash seedlings on ditch edge. Oak standards amongst tall lime-hornbeam (oak) coppice with sparse hazel hawthorn understorey. Not cut for 60 - 80 yrs. Oaks perhaps 100 - 120 yrs. Sparse field layer (but many dead bluebell heads). Dense litter. Stand Type 9A. Merlewood Plot Type 10 NVC Type W10.
SOIL Organic Matter Layers Colour Texture Structure Drainage Depth pH	0-4 cm dark brown, humus stained, clay A1. 5-15cm grey brown clay slight mottling. pH 4.4.

Location	Grid reference	Region	Author

Site and vegetation description	Date	Sample no.

	Altitude		Slope
		m	o

	Aspect		Soil depth
		o	cm

	Stand area		Sample area
	m x	m	m x	m

Layers: mean height

m	m	cm	mm

Layers: cover

%	%	%	%

Geology

Species list

Soil profile

Appendix 4

Main classification systems

Stand Type classification
Merlewood Plot Type classification
National Vegetation Classification
The integration of the NVC with
the NCC's woodland survey programmes

Stand Type classification

Over 700 records from 30 x 30 m (900 m^2) plots placed subjectively in uniform stands in ancient semi-natural woods were examined by Peterken. By inspection these were split into 12 "Stand Groups" according to the presence or absence in the plot, as long-established individuals, of 11 woody species; seedlings, saplings and obviously planted trees were ignored for this purpose. A key to these groups is given below. The groups were further subdivided, on the basis of additional tree and shrub species or site conditions (soil texture, pH and drainage), to give a total of 39 "Stand Types". The subdivisions of Stand Groups 3 (ash-hazel stands) and 6 (oak-birch stands) are shown as examples.

Key to the Stand Groups

(from Peterken 1980; the classification is more fully described in Peterken 1981.)

In this key "present" means that the species occurs as adult or maturing trees or as coppice, is not obviously planted and is not likely to be descended by natural seeding from recently introduced stock. Thus a species which occurs only as seedlings or saplings is deemed to be absent for the purposes of this key. Likewise, planted trees, so-called subspontaneous pines (south of the Highlands) and beech north of the line joining Carmarthen Bay to the Wash should be ignored when using this key.

1   One or more of the following genera present:
Alnus, Fagus, Carpinus, Ulmus or Pinus. 2
All the above genera absent. 4

2   Ulmus glabra present, but Alnus, Fagus, Carpinus, Pinus,
U. carpinifolia and U. procera all absent. Group 1
Not as above. 3

3   Alnus present. Group 7
Fagus present. Group 8
Carpinus present. Group 9
Ulmus carpinifolia/U. procera present. Group 10
Pinus present. Group 11
Two or more of the genera present: Intermediate between
                            appropriate groups.

4   Tilia cordata/T. platyphyllos present. 5
Tilia absent. 6

5   Fraxinus present. Group 4
Fraxinus absent. Group 5

6   Acer campestre present. Group 2
Acer campestre absent. 7

7   Fraxinus present. Group 3
Fraxinus absent. 8

8   Quercus present. Group 6
Quercus absent; Betula present. Group 12
Betula absent: Not classifiable by this system.

Group	Name	Group	Name
1	Wych elm-ash stands	7	Alder stands
2	Maple-ash stands	8	Beech stands
3	Ash-hazel stands	9	Hornbeam stands
4	Lime-ash stands	10	Suckering elm stands
5	Lime-oak stands	11	Pine stands
6	Oak-birch stands	12	Birch stands

Subdivision of groups 3 and 6 in the Stand Group key

(a) Group 3 Ash-hazel stands

Stands contain Fraxinus, but not Acer campestre, Alnus, Carpinus, Fagus, Pinus, Tilia or Ulmus. Almost all stands contain Corylus, and most contain Betula, Crataegus monogyna, Lonicera and Quercus.

1 Main associated oak is Q. robur. (Q. petraea is absent or rare.) 2
   Main associated oak is Q. petraea. 3

2 Soils mostly freely-drained, alkaline. Betula rare; some
   calcicole shrubs present. (Rare.) — **Type 3B**
   Soils either poorly-drained/heavy or acid or both. Most
   stands contain Betula, Crataegus monogyna and Lonicera. — **Type 3A**

3 Soils neutral to alkaline, freely-drained and slightly flushed.
   Betula (often B. pubescens) usually common. (Often on lower
   slopes in birch-oak woodland.) — **Type 3D**

(b) Group 6 Birch-oak stands

Stands contain Quercus petraea and/or Q. robur, but not Acer campestre, Alnus, Carpinus, Fagus, Fraxinus, Pinus, Tilia or Ulmus. (Fagus and Pinus may be present as a result of planting in or near the stand, but are not original natural constituents.) Betula, Ilex, Lonicera and Sorbus aucuparia are usually frequent. Soils are mostly light to medium, acid.

1 Site in the "Highland" zone.* 2
   Site in the "Lowland" zone. 4

2 Q. petraea present; Q. robur absent or very rare. 3
   Q. robur frequent; Q. petraea absent. — **Type 6B**∗∗

3 **Type 6A**
   Corylus absent or very rare; most birches B. pubescens.
   Stands poor in species and soils strongly acid. — **Type 6Ab**
   Corylus frequent; Crataegus also frequent. — **Type 6Ac**

4 Q. petraea present; Betula pendula, Ilex, Prunus avium
   often present. — **Type 6C**∗∗
   Q. petraea absent or very rare; Q. robur present. — **Type 6D**∗∗

  * The "Highland" zone is the area to the north and west of the boundary of
     Palaeozoic rocks.
 ∗∗ Types 6B, 6C and 6D may be subdivided in a manner analogous to Type 6A.

Description of a Stand Type (from Peterken 1981)

Hazel-ash woodland (Group 3)

Stands containing <u>Fraxinus</u>, but not <u>Acer campestre</u>, <u>Alnus</u>, <u>Carpinus</u>, <u>Fagus</u>, <u>Pinus</u> <u>sylvestris</u>, <u>Tilia</u> or <u>Ulmus</u>. Almost all these stands contain <u>Corylus</u>, which is often more abundant than <u>Fraxinus</u>. Most stands contain <u>Betula</u>, <u>Crataegus monogyna</u>, <u>Lonicera</u> and <u>Quercus</u>.

Both hazel and ash are catholic species found almost throughout Britain and growing on a wide range of soils. They are present in most other stand groups and abundant in some, but hazel-ash woodland (i.e. without the species characteristic of other groups) occurs mainly in the north and west beyond the ranges of beech, hornbeam, maple and lime and in the southern lowlands on heavy, acid soils beyond the edaphic ranges of wych elm and maple. The main coppice species are ash and hazel, but oak is also commonly found as coppice as well as standards.

The four stand types are based on associated oak species. The pedunculate oak-hazel-ash woods divide conveniently into types on acid, heavy, poorly-drained soils (3A) and neutral-calcareous, freely-drained soils (3B), with few intermediates. The sessile oak-hazel-ash woods also divide into an acid type (3D) and a calcareous type (3C), but both are mainly found on freely-drained soils, and intermediate stands are relatively common. Each stand type can be regarded as an attenuated version of stand types in groups 1, 2 and 4.

Stand type 3A Acid pedunculate oak-hazel-ash woods

Hazel-ash woodland containing <u>Quercus robur</u> growing on acid soils. Most stands contain <u>Crataegus monogyna</u>, <u>Lonicera</u> and one or other <u>Betula</u> species. <u>Q. petraea</u> is rarely present (but see discussion of 3D). Most stands have been managed as hazel-ash coppice with oak standards, but birch and oak are commonly found as coppice (unlike the related type 2A, where oak is rare as coppice). The type occurs mainly on heavy, poorly-drained, acid (pH 4-5) soils, but some stands grow on markedly lighter and often well-drained soils. This difference is the basis of a division into sub-types on heavy (3Aa) and light (3Ab) soils. The former is closely related to type 2A, whereas the light-soil sub-type is a counterpart of type 2B: both tend to occur on sites which are too acid for maple. Both sub-types are found throughout lowland England and on heavy valley soils in adjacent upland districts, but the type is very rare in Scotland.

(a)   Sub-type 3 Aa Heavy soil form
Acid pedunculate oak-hazel-ash woods on loams, silt and clay. The soils are invariably poorly drained and most have a pH between 4.4 and 5.4. This sub-type is widespread in lowland England and Wales, and is especially characteristic of acid clays in the Midlands, East Anglia and the Weald. Typically, towards the east and south, it is distinguished from 3Ab by the greater frequency of <u>Crataegus</u> <u>oxyacanthoides</u>, <u>Rosa</u> spp., <u>Salix</u> spp. and <u>Thelycrania</u> and the rarity of <u>Sambucus</u>. Good examples occur commonly in the Midland clay belt, on boulder clay in eastern counties, on Wadhurst Clay in East Sussex and on plateau deposits on the chalk. In most of these areas the woods are on flat or gently-sloping ground near a plateau, and the associated stand types are 2A, 6Dc, 9A and (in eastern England) 4A. Salcey Forest (Bucks and Northants) is a good example which was planted as oak high forest in the early 19th century. Some of the most western examples are so distinct in floristic terms that they may merit a separate sub-type, in which <u>Hedera</u> and <u>Ilex</u> are common; <u>Populus tremula</u>, <u>Prunus spinosa</u>, <u>Rosa canina</u> and <u>Thelycrania</u> are absent or rare; and the only birch recorded is <u>B. pubescens</u>. Good examples occur at Ashen Copse (Somerset), Pen-Gelly Forest (Pembs) and in the

Tywi valley near Llandeilo (Carms), where they occur on low-lying ground close to valley alderwoods. In the English lowlands, type 3Aa can be regarded as an attenuated form of 2A, 4A and 9A which is transitional to type 6Da, but in the west it seems to be transitional between 7A or 7B on wetter sites and 6Bc or 3D on drier sites. Stands of type 3A are widely scattered across a range of Merlewood types falling mostly between types 5 and 12 inclusive. Klotzli (1970) would include them in his Querco-Fraxinetum.

The field layer is often dominated by Rubus fruticosus, but many other species may be abundant, including Deschampsia cespitosa and Filipendula ulmaria on wetter soils and Holcus mollis on medium-textured soils. Frequent species are Ajuga reptans, Anemone nemorosa, Arum maculatum, Carex sylvatica, Circaea lutetiana, Deschampsia cespitosa, Dryopteris filix-mas, Endymion non-scriptus, Galium aparine, Geum urbanum, Glechoma hederacea, Holcus mollis, Lonicera periclymenum, Luzula pilosa, Mercurialis perennis, Oxalis acetosella, Poa trivialis, Potentilla sterilis, Primula vulgaris, Rubus fruticosus, Stellaria holostea, Veronica chamaedrys and Viola riviniana. In western examples Dryopteris dilatata, Carex remota and Veronica montana are also frequent.

The Merlewood Plot Type classification

This is based on 1,648 plots, each 14.1 x 14.1 m (200 m²), recorded at random points within 103 woods. The woods were selected as a representative sample from an initial list of over 2,000 woods throughout Britain (Bunce & Shaw 1972). Species lists from these plots were subjected to an Indicator Species Analysis (Hill, Bunce & Shaw 1975). This produced 32 "Plot Types". Any plot recorded in the same way as in the original survey can be allocated to one or other of these types by using a dichotomous key (Bunce 1982). Of the 121 species which occur in the key, 18 are tree or shrub species (with no distinction made between seedlings, saplings, mature trees, etc), 87 are other vascular plants and 16 are bryophytes (mostly common species).

A Plot Type description

Plot Type 2

Bromus ramosus/Mercurialis perennis (hairy brome/dog's mercury) type

Vegetation

Key species

Constant species:	Poa trivialis (rough meadow-grass), Urtica dioica (common nettle), Silene dioica (red campion), Fraxinus excelsior (ash), Mercurialis perennis (dog's mercury), Rubus fruticosus (bramble), Hedera helix (ivy), Eurhynchium praelongum
Plot dominants:	Rubus fruticosus (bramble), Mercurialis perennis (dog's mercury), Galeobdolon luteum (yellow archangel), Hedera helix (ivy)
Selective species:	Anthriscus sylvestris (cow parsley), Bromus ramosus (hairy-brome), Ulmus procera (English elm), Campanula trachelium (nettle-leaved bellflower or bats-in-the-belfry), Silene dioica (red campion), Milium effusum (wood millet).
Species groups:	A, B (D)

Canopy and understorey species

Constant trees:
ash, English elm, oak,
sycamore, hawthorn, field maple

Constant saplings:
English elm, ash, sycamore, hawthorn

Constant shrubs:
elder

Trees (basal area):
oak, ash, English elm

Environment

Geographical distribution

Solid geology

ME (NE, SE, SW)

K Marl/Lias, Oolite/Chalk (G, C, A, F)

Altitude (m)	Slope (°)	Rainfall (cm)	Soil pH	LO1
71 (low)	14 (med)	74 (low)	5.5 (med)	12.6 (low)

General description

A type of average occurrence in an average range of site types, with low heterogeneity and a low species complement, most closely related to types 1, 7 and 4. There is usually a low ground cover with much bare ground. The canopy is usually dense, beneath which there is often an understorey.

This type would probably be described as a pedunculate oak-ash woodland growing under moist base-rich conditions. The soils are mainly brown earths, although often with some gleying. The comparable phytosociological association is probably Ulmo-Fraxinetum E. Sjogren ap KL 1973 (Ulmo-Quercetum Tx 1951).

The first five divisions in the key to Merlewood Plot Types (from information supplied by Dr R G H Bunce and fully described in Bunce 1982)

-1 is scored for each species from the left-hand side of the division which is present in the plot and +1 for each species on the right of the division. The net score for the plot determines the next division.

Negative   Positive

Division 1
Circaea lutetiana   Anthoxanthum odoratum
Eurhynchium praelongum   Deschampsia flexuosa
Fraxinus excelsior   Galium saxatile
Geum urbanum   Polytrichum spp.
Mercurialis perennis   Pteridium aquilinum
Score -1 or less   ....To Division 2
Score 0 or more 17

Division 2
Acer campestre   Athyrium filix-femina
Arum maculatum   Dryopteris austriaca
Corylus avellana   Holcus mollis
Mercurialis perennis   Lysimachia nemorum
                                                         Mnium hornum
                                                         Oxalis acetosella

Score -1 or less 3
Score 0 or more 10

Division 3
Acer pseudoplatanus   Brachypodium sylvaticum
Sambucus nigra   Carex sylvatica
Ulmus procera   Corylus avellana
                                                         Crataegus monogyna
                                                         Lonicera periclymenum
                                                         Rubus fruticosus agg.
                                                         Viola riviniana/reichenbachiana

Score 2 or less 4
Score 3 or more 7

Division 4
Endymion non-scriptus   Acer campestre
Fagus sylvatica   Circaea lutetiana .
Hedera helix   Fissidens taxifolius
Rubus fruticosus agg.   Thamnium alopecurum
Silene dioica   Ulmus procera

Score 0 or less 5
Score 1 or more 6

Division 5
Circaea lutetiana   Anthriscus sylvestris
Corylus avellana   Bromus ramosus
Brachythecium rutabulum   Crataegus monogyna
                                                         Heracleum sphondylium
                                                         Poa trivialis/nemoralis
                                                         Silene dioica
                                                         Ulmus procera

Score 1 or less   ....Type 1
Score 2 or more   ....Type 2

National Vegetation Classification
(based on NVC Progress Report 12, Woodlands, by Dr J Rodwell, Lancaster University)

<u>Data collection and analysis</u>

About 2,800 woodland samples were available for analysis, most of them collected anew by project staff, though with some contribution from existing compatible data from the Scottish lowlands, the Scottish Highlands, Skye, Snowdonia, Durham and mire forests and from various localities and woodland types in published papers and in NCC and other reports. Geographical and floristic coverage is very good, though upland conifer plantations are under-represented.

NVC data were collected from plots placed subjectively in uniform stands, using only floristic and structural homogeneity as the criteria for sample placement, and not the presence of particular species or a particular treatment-derived physiognomy or indications of antiquity. The range of variation included is therefore broader than in schemes which have selected samples on these bases: younger secondary woodlands figure prominently and many kinds of plantation are included. Except in the case of very small stands which were recorded in their entirety, woods were sampled with a 50 x 50 m quadrat for trees and shrubs and either a 10 x 10 m or a 4 x 4 m quadrat for the field and ground layers depending on the structural scale.

All vascular plants, bryophytes and larger lichens were recorded and total floristic data were used for computational analysis. The definition of the vegetation types is thus different from that in schemes which have relied primarily or solely on trees and shrubs or just the field and ground layers. Each of the communities is defined by a unique assemblage of species from all these elements; in some, sub-communities are characterised more by differences among the woody plants; in others, this component remains more constant and there is greater variation among the herbs and bryophytes. This is considered to be a real reflection of woodland complexity.

<u>Communities and presentation</u>

Twenty woodland communities have been characterised - six types of mixed deciduous and oak-birch woodland, three kinds of <u>Fagus sylvatica</u> woodland, communities dominated by <u>Taxus baccata</u> or <u>Juniperus communis</u> ssp. <u>communis</u> or <u>Pinus sylvestris</u> or arctic-alpine willows, and seven types of wetter woodland with various mixtures of <u>Alnus glutinosa</u>, <u>Betula pubescens</u> and <u>Salix</u> species. Plantations of exotic conifers are in all cases considered as modified forms of these communities.

Many of these communities contain stands which, though not mature, are still dominated by more or less the same mixtures of canopy species as are characteristic of mature woodlands; some also include coppices where shrubs figure prominently in the woody cover.

In the floristic tables, canopy species are placed first, then understorey species, then field and ground layer species; for each of these components, constants and companions are clearly separated from sub-community differentials and preferentials. Trees and shrubs commonly appear twice in a table, where they are represented in both canopy and understorey, or three times, where seedlings are present in the field layer. This is essential if the complex variation in the woody cover is to be conveyed; it also often gives some clue as to regeneration patterns.

Mixed-deciduous and oak-birch woodlands

Major floristic trends in relation to soils

The major lines of floristic variation detected among the six communities of mixed-deciduous and oak-birch woodlands are best understood initially in relation to soil differences. One pair of woodlands is associated with rendzinas and brown calcareous earths, not always of high surface pH but base-rich and calcareous at least below and with a tendency to develop mull humus. To the other extreme are two communities characteristic of very acid rankers, brown podzolic soils and podzols with mor. Between, there are two kinds of woodlands on brown earths of low base status, sometimes with moder. One complicating factor of great importance is that many of the less extreme brown soils are moist, sometimes by virtue of inherently poor drainage, in other cases because of flushing; so intermediate profiles are often gleys of various kinds.

Floristic responses to this pattern of edaphic variation are complex: they differ somewhat in the lowland south and east and the sub-montane north and west and, among the woody species, they are often masked by the effects of silvicultural treatments (see below). But the basic outline is clear enough. To the more base-rich and calcareous extreme, the Fraxinus-Acer-Mercurialis and Fraxinus-Sorbus-Mercurialis woodlands have Mercurialis perennis as a strongly preferential vernal herb with Geum urbanum, Circaea lutetiana, Sanicula europaea, Viola reichenbachiana, Arum maculatum and Brachypodium sylvaticum among the more frequent associates of the field layer and Fissidens taxifolius, Ctenidium molluscum, Eurhynchium striatum and Thamnobryum alopecurum as common bryophytes. Quite often, however, the soils here are moist, being derived in many cases from calcareous argillaceous bedrocks or clayey superficials or being flushed with base-rich waters. Then a more strictly calcicolous element in the field layer can be overlain by an abundance of such species as Hyacinthoides non-scripta, Anemone nemorosa, Primula vulgaris (or P. elatior in parts of East Anglia), Glechoma hederacea, Ajuga reptans and Lamiastrum galeobdolon. The woody component in these communities is amongst the richest and most diverse of any kind of British woodland. Oak is very frequent, Tilia cordata and Carpinus betulus can figure prominently, and very many stands have been treated as hazel coppice, but the best preferential species are Fraxinus excelsior, elms (both Ulmus glabra and suckering taxa of the procera and carpinifolia sections) and, especially in southern Britain, Acer campestre, Cornus sanguinea, Rhamnus catharticus and Viburnum lantana.

With a shift to more base-poor brown earths, most of the more calcicolous species in the above communities fade in importance. In the Quercus-Pteridium-Rubus and Quercus-Betula-Oxalis woodlands, Tilia, Carpinus and Castanea sativa can be important local dominants in southern Britain, but overall it is the oaks and birches which provide the most consistent components of the canopy. Corylus avellana and the hawthorns remain prominent in the understorey with Ilex aquifolium and Sorbus aucuparia. The characteristic vernal herb is Hyacinthoides (or Anemone on spring-waterlogged soils and in less oceanic areas), but by mid-summer these woodlands often have a thick cover of Pteridium aquilinum with Rubus fruticosus agg. and Lonicera periclymenum or, where they are grazed, a grass-dominated field layer. Holcus mollis is very typical here, and distinctive associates include Silene dioica, Stellaria holostea, Teucrium scorodonia, Luzula pilosa and Digitalis purpurea with, among the bryophytes, Rhytidiadelphus squarrosus, Dicranum scoparium, Hypnum cupressiforme and Hylocomium splendens.

In the absence of virtually all other canopy trees, the oaks and birches further increase their prominence in the Quercus-Betula-Deschampsia and Quercus-Betula-Dicranum woodlands, the two communities of the base-poor edaphic extreme, and Ilex and Sorbus become the commonest understorey species. In the field layer, Pteridium is still a prominent summer plant, though Rubus and especially Hyacinthoides are much reduced. Typical herbs here are Deschampsia flexuosa, Potentilla erecta, Galium saxatile and Melampyrum pratense, but often more prominent are the ericoid sub-shrubs Vaccinium myrtillus and Calluna vulgaris. The bryophyte flora here is often very rich and abundant, especially to the north-west, but, throughout, more calcifugous species like Polytrichum commune, Dicranum majus, Pleurozium schreberi and Rhytidiadelphus loreus are good preferentials.

Climatic contrasts between the south-east and the north-west

In each of the three pairs of mixed-deciduous and oak-birch woodlands, there is a striking pattern of regional replacement of one community by the other in moving from the south and east to the north and west. Although these regional boundaries are roughly coincident, the floristic differences between the south-eastern and north-western woodlands are varied and of diverse cause. By and large, however, it is direct and indirect effects of climate which produce this contrast.

First, there is the influence of temperature. The floristic divide between the regions corresponds roughly with the 26°C mean annual maximum isotherm, and the cooler, cloudier and shorter summers of the north and west adversely affect the sexual reproduction of a number of important species, such that the Continental and Continental Southern elements in the flora of these woodlands are largely confined to the south-eastern communities. This is especially important towards the calcicolous end of the spectrum, where such species as Acer campestre, Cornus, Euonymus, Viburnum lantana, Rhamnus, Arum and Viola reichenbachiana all help separate the Fraxinus-Acer-Mercurialis woodland from its north-western analogue, the Fraxinus-Sorbus-Mercurialis woodland. Other Continental species are a little more catholic in their soil preferences, being confined largely to the south-east but occurring there in both the Fraxinus-Acer-Mercurialis woodland and its counterpart on more base-poor brown earths, the Quercus-Pteridium-Rubus woodland; Tilia cordata and Carpinus betulus fall into this category and, among the herbs, Lamiastrum galeobdolon and Euphorbia amygdaloides. Conversely, there are some Continental Northern and Northern Montane species which help give a positive definition to north-western woodlands. Again, these are more numerous towards the calcicolous extreme, where Prunus padus, Rubus saxatilis, Actaea spicata, Trollius europaeus, Crepis paludosa and Cirsium helenioides can figure, but Trientalis europaeus is very characteristic of some more calcifugous woodlands to the north-west.

Second, there is rainfall, responses to variations in which reinforce the major regional distinction in woodland floristics. In general, the boundary between the south-eastern and north-western communities coincides with the 1,000 mm isohyet. This makes for a much stronger tendency towards leaching in the north-west, the impact of which is accentuated by the predominance in this region of pervious arenaceous bedrocks. This difference plays a major part in the switch that can be seen in all the pairs of communities from Quercus robur and Betula pendula as the predominant oak and birch of the south-eastern woodlands to Q. petraea and B. pubescens in the north-west, though this separation becomes less obvious the more acid the soils are and, in the case of the oaks, has been much affected by treatment.

One other effect of the predominance of leaching to the north-west is the marked transgression of more calcifugous herbs and bryophytes (like Potentilla erecta, Galium saxatile, Deschampsia flexuosa, Hylocomium splendens, Pleurozium schreberi and Dicranum majus) on to the middle ground of woodland variation, represented by the Quercus-Betula-Oxalis woodland; such plants are generally rare in the south-eastern analogue to this community, the Quercus-Pteridium-Rubus woodland. Indeed, in extreme climatic conditions, these species can be represented very sporadically in the most calcicolous of the north-western communities, the Fraxinus-Sorbus-Mercurialis woodland. This community is maintained somewhat against the odds in the north-west, being locally distributed on limestones or often related to flushing with base-rich waters, which offsets the effects of leaching. It is close floristically to the more calcicolous of our alder woods, contrasting markedly with much of the south-eastern Fraxinus-Acer-Mercurialis woodland.

Two further related climatic features serve to sharpen up these regional differences. One is that, though the soils to the north-west are more consistently free-draining and leached, they are kept generally moist throughout the year by the high rainfall; in particular, they are free from marked droughting in summer, which can affect even the more ill-draining lowland soils. One good indication of this is the transgression across much of the range of north-western woodlands of Corylus, Viola riviniana and Oxalis acetosella which, in the south-east, tend to be confined to heavier, base-rich soils. Another is the increasing prominence, in moving to the north and west, of Acer pseudoplatanus which, though an introduction to Britain, has become most frequent in woodlands in exactly the same climatic conditions as it favours in its natural European range.

Finally, the consistency of surface and atmospheric moisture in the north-west (where there are generally at least 160 wet days per year) encourages a greater profusion of ferns and bryophytes in all the woodlands there, an abundance which is often accentuated by the rockier topography of the sub-montane zone with its local enhancement of cool, humid conditions and provision of a multiplicity of niches. Different groups of species mark out each of the north-western woodland types: among the ferns, Dryopteris dilatata tends to increase throughout, but, towards the calcicolous end of the range, Phyllitis scolopendrium and Polystichum spp. are very characteristic, with Blechnum spicant preferential at the opposite extreme. Among the bryophytes, the regional differences are best seen in the calcifugous communities, where mosses and liverworts provide the major distinction between the south-eastern Quercus-Betula-Deschampsia woodland and the north-western Quercus-Betula-Dicranum woodland, though in the Pennines the transition between these two is blurred by the demise of bryophytes as a result of the long history of atmospheric pollution.

The effects of silvicultural treatments

Variations in soil and climate provide the best basis for understanding the major floristic differences between and within our mixed-deciduous and oak-birch woodlands. But, very often, these differences are overlain by the effects of silvicultural treatments. Treatments operate within the general constraints that edaphic and climatic conditions impose, though they do not always work in the same direction. Sometimes, treatments sharpen up patterns of floristic variation related to natural environmental variation; often they work against them, blurring differences. Most obviously, treatments such as the removal or planting of different timber trees or the selective coppicing of underwood crops can result in a great diversity of woody cover in what is really the same kind of woodland; or, conversely, the same treatment can produce identical timber or underwood covers in what are actually different woodland communities. The sections on synonymy and affinities in each community description indicate correspondences to and differences from the woodland types recognised in the schemes of Peterken and Rackham, and numerous notes throughout point up possible areas of integration of the different approaches to woodland classification.

Although the effects of treatments on the floristics of these woodlands are rarely sufficiently obvious to characterise even sub-communities, their impact is dealt with in detail in the community descriptions. Special attention has been given to features like the artificially low cover of oak in many kinds of coppiced woodland (particularly in the Fraxinus-Acer-Mercurialis and Quercus-Pteridium-Rubus woodlands) and to the part that planting has played in local balances between Quercus robur and Q. petraea (especially noticeable in the Quercus-Pteridium-Rubus woodland and in eastern Scottish stands of the Quercus-Betula-Oxalis and Quercus-Betula-Dicranum woodlands); the impact of coppicing for hazel, ash, maple, lime, hornbeam and chestnut (very obvious in the Fraxinus-Acer-Mercurialis and/or the Quercus-Pteridium-Rubus woodlands) and for oak (important in the Quercus-Betula-Oxalis and Quercus-Betula-Dicranum woodlands); the distinctive post-coppice floras which develop in the different communities; the results of coppice neglect; and the effects of replanting or the establishment of new plantations with either the natural woody dominants or other hardwoods or softwoods.

One other type of treatment (or important kind of incidental occurrence where herbivores get into unenclosed woodlands) is grazing and browsing by stock and wild mammals. The effects of such predation are widespread, various and often considerable. They are locally important where south-eastern communities (notably the Quercus-Pteridium-Rubus and Quercus-Betula-Deschampsia woodlands) occur in lowland wood-pasture landscapes of forests, parks and commons, and much more consistently obvious among the north-western communities (especially the Quercus-Betula-Oxalis and Quercus-Betula-Dicranum woodlands) where grazing is prevalent along the sub-montane fringe. Here grazing tends to produce a floristic convergence between these communities on less extreme soils by eliminating sensitive preferentials and favouring a spread both of tolerant grasses and dicotyledons and, with the lack of vigorous competition in the sward, of bryophytes. Such responses help to reinforce the climatically-related contrast between these woodlands and their south-eastern analogues.

Beech and yew woodlands

The scheme recognises a separate suite of three woodlands in which Fagus sylvatica is the overwhelming canopy dominant. In general terms, these communities are beech analogues of the three south-eastern mixed deciduous and oak-birch woodlands, one strongly calcicolous, one markedly calcifugous and one in between, so the classification preserves, by and large, the traditional English view of these communities and the Continental sub-division of Fagion alliance. But the communities have a more restricted distribution, being centred in what seems to be the native British range of Fagus and represented locally elsewhere by beech plantations (often floristically indistinguishable); and, of course, the great shading power of this tree and the intense root-competition it exerts often produce an impoverished version of the particular field and ground layers. Indeed, in extreme situations, there can be considerable difficulty in telling the different beech woodlands apart until gaps or clearings occur. Among associated woody species, there tends to be an increase throughout in more shade-tolerant trees, like Ilex and to a lesser extent Taxus baccata, which can create an impression of overall similarity.

The proportion of Fagus in our more southerly woods is very variable, so the dividing line between the beech woodlands and the analogous mixed deciduous and oak-birch types can sometimes look rather ill-defined. Towards the more calcicolous end of the spectrum, separation is a little easier because, though the woodlands are floristically very similar, they show a fairly clear environmental separation: essentially, the Fagus-Mercurialis woodland is an edaphic replacement for the Fraxinus-Acer-Mercurialis woodland on more free-draining calcareous soils within the native range of beech, most notably on the scarps of the southern Chalk. On moving on to more base-poor brown earths, this kind of distinction becomes less obvious, though still the Fagus-Rubus woodland tends to be a community of permeable profiles, the Quercus-Pteridium-Rubus woodland one of heavier soils. By the time one reaches the most acid soils, which are uniformly free-draining, the situation is much more difficult, and almost infinitely variable mixtures of beech, oak and birch can be found over field and ground layers which vary only with the differences of shade under the diverse canopy mosaic.

Successional interpretations of these kinds of gradations should be undertaken with some caution. There is no doubt that each of the mixed deciduous and oak-birch woodlands can function as seral precursors to their beech analogues and also that, once Fagus has become pre-eminent, it is a very uncompromising canopy dominant. However, whether these different kinds of beech woodlands are inevitable climax forests is not so clear: beech fruits erratically and spreads with some difficulty when unaided. So, in circumstances where edaphic conditions are equally favourable to woodlands with or without Fagus, there may be some quite natural cyclical replacements through time, one type repeatedly giving way to the other.

Even within the native British range of beech, the communities it dominates are often of planted origin or severely affected by treatment. Coppice is rare (though it was probably more common in the past) but timber extraction is still widespread. In the Chilterns, many stands still bear signs of management under the selection system, though cutting is now usually on a clear-fell or shelterwood regime and replanting often involves the use of beech-conifer mixtures. Planted stands beyond the natural range can generally be readily incorporated into the relevant beech community, though a few far-flung (but long-established) Scottish plantations are best placed in the Quercus-Betula-Oxalis woodland.

Taxus baccata is a characteristic associate of Fagus in all three kinds of beech woodland, forming part of a second tier of shade-tolerant trees and being especially prominent in areas like the New Forest and on the Chalk of south-east England. But, in certain circumstances, especially on warm and sunny south-facing slopes over shallow limestone soils, it can pre-empt beech and become dominant in a very distinctive Taxus baccata woodland. Floristically, such vegetation can be seen as a yew analogue of the calcicolous south-eastern woodlands, though extremely dense shade and the very inhospitable edaphic environment make this community one of the most species-poor of all our woodlands. Nonetheless, these yew woods are among the finest in Europe and provide the usual context for Buxus sempervirens in what are probably native British localities.

Taxus grows very well far to the north of the main area of distribution of the yew woods and is a perfectly natural feature in many stands of the Fraxinus-Acer-Mercurialis woodland on the Carboniferous Limestone of Wales, Derbyshire and the Pennines and around Morecambe Bay: indeed, there is good circumstantial evidence that it can mark out less-modified or relict stands of this community towards its north-western limit, where many woodlands are of relatively recent origin. Although Taxus can attain some measure of local abundance here, such stands are retained within the Fraxinus-Acer-Mercurialis woodland.

Pine and juniper woodlands and arctic-alpine willow scrub

Planted Pinus sylvestris figures as a replacement canopy tree in a variety of mixed-deciduous and oak-birch woodlands, both in the south-east and the north-west, and it has also been widely planted within the region of natural beech-dominance. In Scotland, however, within what is presumed to be its present natural range, pine dominates in a distinctive Pinus-Hylocomium woodland. In many ways, this community can be regarded as an analogue, on similarly base-poor soils, of the Quercus-Betula-Dicranum woodland. Ericoid sub-shrubs and calcifuge bryophytes figure prominently in the associated flora, though here they are joined by Vaccinium vitis-idaea and Ptilium crista-castrensis and a striking contingent of rare Northern Montane and Continental Northern plants such as Goodyera repens, Listera cordata, Linnaea borealis and wintergreens. The community extends a little way on to more fertile soils, now generally occupied in this region by the Quercus-Betula-Oxalis woodland, and in wetter areas has a prominent Sphagnum component in the ground layer, which brings it close floristically to the Betula-Molinia mire woodland. Although pine plantations in this part of Scotland can acquire many elements of the typical associated flora and be included here, there seems little doubt that the remaining distribution of the community represents in part a direct, though fragmentary, inheritance of the prevalence of pine in the cooler parts of Scotland through the Post-Glacial Period.

Evidence suggests that, in the past, the canopies of our native pine forests were much more mixed, with birch and Juniperus communis ssp. communis represented much more consistently than at present as an integral component of the woody cover. These species can still figure locally in close association with the Pinus-Hylocomium woodland, and juniper also occurs in the Quercus-Betula-Oxalis and Quercus-Betula-Dicranum woodlands of eastern Scotland, but, very often now, a distinct Juniperus-Oxalis scrubby woodland persists in this region as a seral community which, for one reason or another, does not progress to mature forest. Overall, this community is analogous to the Quercus-Betula-Oxalis woodland, but one sub-community extends its cover on to more markedly acid soils, another on to flushed profiles which can be quite base-rich. Centred in the more continental parts of eastern Scotland, Trientalis europaeus, Anemone nemorosa and Rhytidiadelphus triquetrus are common and some Continental Northern and Northern Montane rarities can also occur, helping to place the community phytosociologically with the Pinus-Hylocomium woodland in the Vaccinio-Picetea. The floristic character of the Juniperus-Oxalis woodland is thus very different from that of the seral scrub in which juniper can figure in the southern lowlands of England.

The Juniperus-Oxalis woodland is typically a high-altitude community and, in some places, it may represent a sub-alpine climax scrub. In scattered localities through the southern and central Highlands of Scotland it is replaced on wetter and more mesotrophic soils at high altitudes by the Salix-Luzula scrub, provided that there is freedom from grazing to allow the development of the low cover of arctic-alpine willows (S. lapponum, S. myrsinites, S. lanata, S. arbuscula and S. reticulata) and lush tall-herbs, ferns and ericoid sub-shrubs. Largely, now, this community is restricted to isolated and inaccessible banks and ledges and, with wide scattering of the dioecious willows, it does not seem readily able to colonise any new suitable sites. Here, it is often replaced by tall-herb vegetation of the Betulo-Adenostyletea, in which class it can also be placed, perhaps in the Salicion arbusculae.

Wet woodlands with alder, birch and willows

Seven types of woodland are characterised by the dominance in the canopy of various mixtures of Alnus glutinosa, Betula pubescens and Salix spp. in habitats where the wetness of the ground is (or recently has been) the overriding element in the environment. For the most part, floristic variation among these communities can be understood in terms of interactions between the amount of soil moisture, the degree of base-richness and the trophic state of the system. Often, the combination of the different values of these variables favoured by each of the woodland types is associated with a particular kind of mire or flush, and the distribution of the communities is frequently a reflection of the occurrence of these different site types. In the early stages of colonisation, there is often a chance element in the assortment of woody species that invade; as the woodland matures, the canopy tends to equilibrate and its increasing closure and the gradual process of terrestralisation exert effects on the preceding swamp or mire vegetation.

Regional climatic influence on the floristics and distribution of these woodlands is not so apparent as among the drier forests, though some communities show an Atlantic influence (with such species as Carex paniculata, C. laevigata and Oenanthe crocata) and in others there is a Continental Northern element (Salix pentrandra, S. nigricans, Carex elongata, Crepis paludosa, Circaea x intermedia, Lysimachia thyrsiflora and Peucedanum palustre). Neither is silvicultural treatment of such importance here: drier stands of a number of communities have sometimes been coppiced (notably for alder) and one kind of osier-dominated Alnus-Urtica woodland is still commercially cropped in some areas. In general, however, human influence has been felt through such activities as draining and reclamation, which have greatly reduced the extent of many communities or induced changes by lowering the water table; more locally, the neglect of mowing for marsh crops has allowed some secondary spread.

Two communities are especially associated with primary colonisation of swamps. Where the waters are fairly base-rich and eutrophic, favouring the accumulation of fen peat in topogenous mires and valley fens and below springs, the Alnus-Carex paniculata woodland is very characteristic. This is our major Alnion glutinosae woodland in Britain, representing a more Atlantic replacement of Continental swamp forests with Carex elongata and having a rich associated flora inherited from the preceding swamps, with large sedges like C. paniculata, C. acutiformis and C. elata, herbs such as Filipendula ulmaria, Eupatorium cannabinum, Iris pseudacorus, Valeriana officinalis, V. dioica, Angelica sylvestris, Lycopus europaeus, Lythrum salicaria, Lysimachia vulgaris and, in Broadland, Peucedanum palustre and ferns including Dryopteris dilatata, Athyrium filix-femina, Thelypteris palustris and Osmunda regalis. The Alnus-Carex woodland has a fairly wide distribution on mire remnants throughout the English lowlands, forming classic swamp carr. It may not always progress to drier forest but, around open waters, show a cyclical pattern of development and decay.

The counterpart of this community in very wet poor-fen systems, where there is a somewhat different (though little understood) balance of base-status and trophic levels, is the Salix-Carex rostrata woodland. This is essentially a northern sub-montane community, its distribution reflecting the occurrence of less acidic and oligotrophic basin mires, where it typically colonises a mat of such species as Carex rostrata, Menyanthes trifoliata, Potentilla palustris, Equisetum fluviatile, Valeriana spp., Filipendula ulmaria, Angelica sylvestris, Geum rivale, Crepis paludosa, Caltha palustris, Cardamine pratensis and large Calliergon spp. and Mniaceae. The sites are frequently isolated and stands often lack Alnus and have a promiscuous mixture of Salix species, among which S. pentandra is generally prominent.

Base-rich and moderately eutrophic systems where the influence of the water table is still strong but not sufficient to maintain swamp typically have the Salix-Betula-Phragmites woodland, the classic fen carr of terrestrialising mires with fen peat, though now often found as a secondary development on abandoned mowing-marsh. It shares many species with the Alnus-Carex woodland, though here the commonest monocotyledon is Phragmites australis rather than one of the bulky swamp sedges and, in secondary stands, the floristics of the field layer often reflect a lasting influence of different cutting regimes. Again, the isolation of stands can have some effect on the pattern of colonisation by woody plants, such that species which are usually no more than occasional (Frangula alnus and Rhamnus catharticus at Wicken, for example) can attain great local prominence.

In more markedly eutrophic systems, these immature Salicion cinereae woodlands and the Alnus-Carex woodland are replaced by Salicion albae communities, all our examples of which are grouped in this scheme in a single compendious Alnus-Urtica woodland. This can develop in fen-peat systems where there has been some degree of enrichment through substrate disturbance or eutrophication of the waters, but it includes all those woodland types which develop naturally on rich accumulating alluvium in more mature river valleys and around silting water bodies. Although Alnus and Salix cinerea can be prominent colonisers in such places, a variety of other Salix species can come to dominate, including, in immature stands and osier beds, S. viminalis, S. triandra and S. purpurea and, on wet river terraces, S. fragilis. The field layer is much less species-rich than in typical swamp and fen woodlands, being typically dominated by an assemblage of more nutrient-demanding herbs, notably Urtica dioica and Galium aparine.

Most of these communities show clear floristic transitions to drier mixed-deciduous woodlands, but in the Salix-Betula-Phragmites woodland (and, to a lesser extent, the Salix-Carex woodland) there is evidence of a successional divergence to more calcifugous vegetation, with a shift away from Alnus and Salix dominance towards Betula pubescens and an appearance of less-demanding Sphagna (S. recurvum, S. palustre, S. squarrosum and S. fimbriatum) around what seem to be ombrogenous nuclei isolated from the influence of the ground water table. Such a trend continues into the Betula-Molinia woodland where these Sphagna, along with Molinia caerulea, become a more or less consistent feature beneath rather open birch covers on moist and moderately acid peaty soils. As well as occurring on raised areas within flood-plain and basin mires, this community can also be found colonising the fringes of extensive blanket mires and in more base-poor valley mires. In all these situations, the same general balance of soil conditions is marked by a poverty of rich-fen herbs and the presence of field-layer species more typical of wet heath and small-sedge and Juncus mires.

Certain types of Betula-Molinia woodland extend the cover of these communities into markedly soligenous sites. In more base-rich flushes with strongly-gleyed mineral soils, the counterpart of the Betula-Molinia woodland is the Alnus-Fraxinus-Lysimachia woodland. Here, Alnus, Salix cinerea and Betula all retain prominence, with the field and ground layers both showing the influence of consistent flushing, with species such as Lysimachia nemorum, Filipendula ulmaria, Athyrium filix-femina, Ranunculus repens, Chrysosplenium oppositifolium, Brachythecium rivulare and Pellia epiphylla and bulky dominants like Juncus effusus, Deschampsia cespitosa, Carex pendula and C. remota. This community has a strongly western and northern distribution, reflecting the occurrence of slope flushes along the upland fringes, and it provides one locus for plants like Carex laevigata and Crepis paludosa. It grades floristically to the Fraxinus-Sorbus-Mercurialis woodland and, like it, is best placed in the Alno-Ulmion alliance.

Finally, among these wetter woodlands, there is the Salix--Galium woodland, containing stands in which S. cinerea is the sole woody dominant over mixtures of species like Juncus effusus, Mentha aquatica and Galium palustre, generally without any swamp or fen monocotyledons. It is typical of waterlogged mineral soils of only moderate base-status and nutrient-richness in field hollows, around dune slacks and on cliff-top flushes where, for one reason or another, Alnus invasion is restricted. In exposed and isolated sites, it may attain some measure of stability.

The integration of the National Vegetation Classification with the NCC's woodland survey programmes (a preliminary note)

The NVC provides the NCC with a powerful floristic classification which will gradually be adopted as a basis for our woodland survey and evaluation work. It may however take several years for this process to be completed, and a careful training programme is required. The most experience so far with the system lies in Scotland, where it has been used by the Scottish Field Unit.

Once the system has been learnt, relatively little change in our procedures is required; the standard record cards can still be used, with or without separate sub-site recording, except that the vegetation maps produced and descriptions of areas will be in NVC terms. These may be supported by NVC quadrat data where necessary (or in some cases by old-style quadrat records).

The difficulty lies in the change-over period as we learn

(a)   how to recognise what constitutes a "homogeneous" stand in NVC terms and become familiar with the use of the tables, descriptions and keys to classify these;

(b)   what are the minimum areas and degrees of vegetation difference that are worth distinguishing either because they represent a change in NVC type (community or sub-community) or because they are variations which are important in conservation terms even though they do not represent a change of NVC type.

Perhaps inevitably, surveyors using the NVC system in the next few years will have to do far more quadrat recording, to check that their type identification is correct, than may be necessary later when there is greater familiarity with the system. So, for example, where an area is encountered which cannot be assigned immediately to its NVC sub-community, surveyors should quickly list the ground flora species at five points within the area (considering an area of roughly 5 x 5 m at each point) as well as species in the tree and shrub community around each point or over the whole area (where the area is small). This information can be used to assess species frequency within the area and to allocate it to an NVC sub-community by using the key and constancy tables.

References

AHLEN, I. 1981. Identification of Scandinavian bats by their sounds. Uppsala, Swedish University Agricultural Science, Department of Wildlife Ecology (Report 6).

ANDERSON, M. 1979. The development of plant habitats under exotic forest crops. In: Ecology and design in amenity land management, ed. by S.E. Wright and G.P. Buckley, 87-108. Wye, Recreation Ecology Research Group.

ANDERSON, M.C. 1964. Studies of the woodland light climate. I. The photographic computation of light conditions. Journal of Ecology, 52, 27-41.

ANDERSON, M.L. 1967. A history of Scottish forestry. London, Nelson.

ANON. 1974. Survey and monitoring in nature conservation. Unpublished report of combined NCC/ITE study group.

ARCHIBALD, J.F. 1981. Management control and stand structure monitoring on woodland nature reserves. Peterborough, Nature Conservancy Council (unpublished).

ARNOLD, H.R. 1984. Distribution maps of the mammals of the British Isles. Huntingdon, Monks Wood Experimental Station, Biological Records Centre.

ASH, J.E., & BARKHAM, J.P. 1976. Changes and variability in the field layer of a coppiced woodland in Norfolk, England. Journal of Ecology, 64, 697-712.

BACKMEROFF, C.E. 1987. Monks Wood NNR: transect recording of trees and shrubs, summer 1985. Peterborough, Nature Conservancy Council (CSD Research Report No. 710).

BANG, P., & DAHLSTROM, P. 1974. Collins guide to animal tracks and signs. London, Collins.

BALL, D.F., & STEVENS, P.A. 1981. The role of ancient woods in conserving undisturbed soils. Biological Conservation, 19, 163-176.

BARKMAN, J.J. 1958. Phytosociology and ecology of cryptogamic epiphytes. Assen, Netherlands, Van Gorcum.

BARNES, R.F.W., & TAPPER, S.C. 1985. A method for counting hares by spotlight. Journal of Zoology, London, 205, 273-276.

BIBBY, C.J., PHILLIPS, B.N., & SEDDON, A.J.E. 1985. Birds of restocked conifer plantations in Wales. Journal of Applied Ecology, 22, 619-33.

BIBBY, C.J., & ROBINS, M. 1985. An exploratory analysis of species and community relationships with habitat in western oak woods. In: Birds census and atlas studies. Proceedings of the VIII International Conference on Bird Census and Atlas work, 1983, ed. by K. Taylor, R.J. Fuller and P. C. Lack, 255-264. Tring, British Trust for Ornithology.

BIRKS, H.J.B. 1973. Past and present vegetation of the Isle of Skye. Cambridge, Cambridge University Press.

BIRSE, E.L. 1980. Plant communities of Scotland: revised and additional tables. A preliminary phytocoenonia. Aberdeen, Macaulay Institute for Soil Research. (Soil Survey of Scotland Bulletin No. 4).

BIRSE, E.L., & ROBERTSON, J.S. 1976. Plant communities and soils of the lowland and southern upland regions of Scotland. Aberdeen., Macaulay Institute for Soil Research. (Soil Survey of Scotland Monograph).

BOWEN, H.J.M. 1976. The lichen flora of Dorset. Lichenologist, 8, 1-33.

BOWEN, H.J.M. 1980. A lichen flora of Berkshire, Buckinghamshire and Oxfordshire. Lichenologist, 12, 199-237.

BOYCOTT, A.E. 1934. The habits of land mollusca in Britain. Journal of Ecology, 22, 1-38.

BRITISH LICHEN SOCIETY. 1982. Survey and assesment of epiphytic lichen habitats. Peterborough, Nature Conservancy Council (CSD Research Report No. 384).

BROOKS, A. 1980. Woodlands. Wallingford, British Trust for Conservation Volunteers.

BROWN, A.H.F., & OOSTERHUIS, L. 1981. The role of buried seed in coppice woods. Biological Conservation, 21, 19-38.

BUCKING, W. 1986. Study of vegetation changes in natural forest reserves in south-west Germany. In: Forest dynamics research in Western and Central Europe, ed. by J. Fanta, 231-241. Wageningen, Pudoc for IUFRO.

BUCKING, W., KATZLER, W., LANGE, E., REINHARDT, W., & WEISHAAR, H. 1986. Methods for documenting succession in forests as developed and applied in natural forest reserves in south-west Germany. In: Forest dynamics research in Western and Central Europe, ed. by J. Fanta, 265-273. Wageningen, Pudoc for IUFRO.

BUNCE, F.M., & BUNCE, R.G.H. 1977. Survey of the broadleaved woodlands of the Yorkshire Dales National Park. Yorkshire Dales National Park (unpublished).

BUNCE, R.G.H. 1981. British woodlands in a European context. In: Forest and woodland ecology, ed. by F.T. Last and A.S. Gardiner, 7-11. Cambridge, Institute of Terrestrial Ecology.

BUNCE, R.G.H. 1982. A field key for classifying British woodland vegetation. Cambridge, Institute of Terrestrial Ecology.

BUNCE, R.G.H., BARR, C.J., & WHITTAKER, H. 1983. A stratification system for ecological mapping. In: Ecological mapping from ground, air and space, ed. by R.M. Fuller, 39-46. Huntingdon, Institute of Terrestrial Ecology (ITE Symposium No. 10).

BUNCE, R.G.H., & JEFFERS, J.N.R., eds. 1977. Native pinewoods of Scotland. Cambridge, Institute of Terrestrial Ecology.

BUNCE, R.G.H., MUNRO, R.C., & PARR, T.W. 1979. Deciduous woodland survey of Scotland. (ITE contract report). Peterborough, Nature Conservancy Council (CSD Research Report No. 250).

BUNCE, R.G.H., & SHAW, M.W. 1972. Classifying woodlands for nature conservation. Forestry and British Timber, 1, 23-25.

BUNCE, R.G.H., & SHAW, M.W. 1973. A standardised procedure for ecological survey. Journal of Environmental Management, 1, 239-258.

BURN, A.M. 1986. Development of a method for monitoring lowland wetland vegetation and fen carr at Llangloffan Fen, Pembs. Welsh Field Unit report. Bangor, Nature Conservancy Council (unpublished).

BURNHAM, C.P. 1980. The soils of England and Wales. Field Studies, 5, 349-363.

CAMERON, R.A.D. 1980. Stand structure, species composition and succession in some Shropshire woods. Field Studies, 5, 289-306.

CHANIN, P.R.F., & JEFFERIES, D.J. 1978. The decline of the otter Lutra lutra L. in Britain: an analysis of hunting records and discussion of causes. Linnean Society. Biological Journal, 10, 305-328.

CLAPHAM, A.R., TUTIN, T.G., & WARBURG, G.F. 1962. Flora of the British Isles. 2nd ed. Cambridge, Cambridge University Press.

CLAPHAM, A.R., TUTIN, T.G., & WARBURG, G.F. 1983. Excursion flora of the British Isles. 3rd ed. Cambridge, Cambridge University Press.

CLARKE, R. 1986. The handbook of ecological monitoring. Oxford, Clarendon Press.

COLEBOURN, P. 1983. Hampshire's countryside heritage - ancient woodland. Winchester, Hampshire County Council.

COLEMAN, A., & SHAW, J. 1980. Field mapping manual. London, Second Land Utilisation Survey of Britain.

COTTAM, G., & CURTIS, J.T. 1956. The method of making rapid surveys of woods by means of pairs of randomly selected trees. Ecology, 30, 101-104.

CURTIS, D.J., & BIGNAL, E.M. 1985. Quantitative description of vegetation physiognomy using vertical quadrats. Vegetatio, 63, 97-104.

CURTIS, L.F., COURTNEY, F.M., & TRUDGILL, S. 1976. Soils in the British Isles. London, Longman.

DAY, P. 1986. Broadleaved woodland in the North Wales Region: survey, evaluation and site selection. Bangor, Nature Conservancy Council (unpublished).

DAWKINS, H.C., & FIELD, D.R.B. 1978. A long-term surveillance system for British woodland vegetation. Oxford, Commonwealth Forestry Institute (CFI Occasional Papers No. 1).

DOBSON, F.S. 1979. Lichens. An illustrated guide. Richmond, Richmond Publishing.

DON, B.A.C. 1985. The use of drey counts to estimate grey squirrel populations. Journal of Zoology, London, 205, 282-286.

DUNSTONE, N., & BIRKS, J.D.S. 1983. Activity budget and habitat usage by coastal living mink (Mustela vison Schreber). Acta Zoologica Fennica, 174, 189-191.

EDWARDS, P.N., & CHRISTIE, J.M. 1981. Yield models for forest management. London, HMSO (Forestry Commission Booklet 48).

ELTON, C. 1966. The pattern of animal communities. London, Methuen.

EMLEN, J.T. 1967. A rapid method for assessing arboreal cover. Ecology, 48, 158-160.

ENGLAND FIELD UNIT. 1982. A survey of Orlestone Forest, Kent. Peterborough, Nature Conservancy Council (unpublished).

EVANS, J. 1984. Silviculture of broadleaved woodland. London, HMSO (Forestry Commission Bulletin 62).

EVERETT, S. 1984. Woodland habitat change review. Peterborough, Nature Conservancy Council (CST Note 36).

FALINSKI, J.B. 1986. Vegetation dynamics in temperate lowland primeval forests. The Hague, Junk.

FARR, R. 1974. Commentary. In: Landscape evaluation, a comparison of techniques, ed. by R.S. Crofts and R.U. Cooke. London, Univeristy College London, Department of Geography (Occasional Paper No. 25).

FLOYD, D.A., & ANDERSON, J.A. 1987. A comparison of three methods for estimating plant cover. Journal of Ecology, 75, 221-228.

FORD, E.D., & NEWBOULD, P.J. 1977. The biomass and production of ground vegetation and its relation to tree cover through a deciduous woodland cycle. Journal of Ecology, 65, 201-212.

FORESTRY COMMISSION. 1983. Census of woodlands and trees (Herefordshire). Edinburgh, Forestry Commission.

FORESTRY COMMISSION. 1985a. The policy for broadleaved woodland. Edinburgh, Forestry Commission (Policy & Procedure Paper No. 5).

FORESTRY COMMISSION. 1985b. Management guidelines for broadleaved woodland. Edinburgh, Forestry Commission.

FRENKEL, R.E., & HARRISON, C.M. 1974. An assessment of the usefulness of phytosociological and numerical classificatory methods for the community biogeographer. Journal of Biogeography, 1, 27-56.

FULLER, R.J. 1982. Bird habitats in Britain. Calton, Poyser.

FULLER, R.J., & TAYLOR, K. 1983. Breeding birds and woodland management in some Lincolnshire limewoods. (NCC/BTO contract report). Peterborough, Nature Conservancy Council (unpublished).

FULLER, R.M., ed. 1983. Ecological mapping from ground, air and space. Huntingdon, Institute of Terrestrial Ecology. (ITE Symposium No. 10).

GAME, M., & PETERKEN, G.F. 1984. Nature reserve selection strategies in the woodlands of central Lincolnshire, England. Biological Conservation, 29, 157-181.

GILBERT, O.L. 1977. Lichen conservation in Britain. In: Lichen ecology, ed. by M.R.D. Seaward, 415-436. London, Academic Press.

GILBERT, O.L. 1980. Lichen flora of Northumberland. Lichenologist, 12, 325-395.

GOODFELLOW, S., & PETERKEN, G.F. 1981. A method for survey and assessment of woodlands for nature conservation using maps and species lists: the example of Norfolk woodlands. Biological Conservation, 21, 177-196.

GOOSSENS, R., VAN GENDEREN, J., & DE WULF, R. 1984. Airborne MSS data processing for forest classification. International Journal of Remote Sensing, 5, 939-941.

GREIG-SMITH, P. 1983. Quantitative plant ecology. 3rd ed. Oxford, Blackwell.

GURNELL, J. 1983. Squirrel numbers and the abundance of tree seeds. Mammal Review, 13, 133-148.

GURNELL, J., & FLOWERDEW, J.R. 1982. Live trapping small mammals. A practical guide. Reading, Mammal Society.

HAMILTON, G.J. 1975. Forest mensuration handbook. London, HMSO (Forestry Commission Booklet 39).

HAMMOND, P.M. 1974. Changes in the British Coleopterous fauna. In: The changing flora and fauna of Britain, ed. by D.L. Hawkesworth, 323-369. London, Academic Press.

HARDING, P.T. 1978. An inventory of areas of conervation value for the invertebrate fauna of the mature timber habitat. (ITE contract report). Peterborough, Nature Conservancy Council (CSD Research Report No. 160).

HARDING, P.T., & ROSE, F. 1986. Pasture-woodlands in lowland England. Huntingdon, Institute of Terrestrial Ecology.

HARLEY, J.B. 1975. Ordnance Survey maps - a descriptive manual. Southampton, Ordnance Survey.

HARLEY, J.B. 1979. The Ordnance Survey and land use mapping. Norwich, Geobooks.

HAWKSWORTH, D.L., & SEAWARD, M.R.D. 1977. Lichenology in the British Isles 1598-1975. Richmond, Richmond Publishing Company.

HENDERSON, D.M., & MANN, D. 1984. Birches. Royal Society of Edinburgh. Proceedings, B, 85, 1-213.

HIGHLAND REGIONAL COUNCIL. 1985. Amenity woodland survey. Inverness, Higland Regional Council (Planning Department Information Paper 7).

HILL, M.O. 1979a. The development of a flora in even-aged plantations. In: The ecology of even-aged plantations, ed. by E.D. Ford, D.C. Malcolm and J. Atterson, 175-192. Cambridge, Institute of Terrestrial Ecology.

HILL, M.O. 1979b. TWINSPAN. A FORTRAN program for arranging multivariate data in an ordered two way table by classification of the individuals and the attributes. Ithaca, New York, Cornell University.

HILL, M.O., BUNCE, R.G.H., & SHAW, M.W. 1975. Indicator species analysis, a divisive polythetic method of classification and its application to a study of the native pine-woods of Scotland. Journal of Ecology, 63, 597-613.

HILL, M.O., & JONES, E.W. 1978. Vegetation changes resulting from the afforestation of rough grazings in Caeo Forest, South Wales. Journal of Ecology, 66, 433-456.

HILL, M.O., & RADFORD, G.L. 1986. Register of permanent vegetation plots. Huntingdon, Institute of Terrestrial Ecology, Monks Wood Experimental Station.

HODGSON, J.M. 1974. Soil survey field methods handbook. Harpenden, Soil Survey (Technical Monograph 4).

HORRILL, A.D., & SYKES, J.M. 1975. Monitoring studies in north-west Scotland: Glen Nant SSSI. (ITE contract report). Peterborough, Nature Conservancy Council (CSD Research Report No. 12).

HORRILL, A.D., & SYKES, J.M. 1976. Monitoring studies in north-west Scotland: Glasdrum. (ITE contract report). Peterborough, Nature Conservancy Council (CSD Research Report No. 80).

HORRILL, A.D., & SYKES, J.M. 1977. Monitoring studies in north-west Scotland: Arriundle. (ITE contract report). Peterborough, Nature Conservancy Council (CSD Research Report No. 96).

HORRILL, A.D., SYKES, J.M., & IDLE, E.T. 1975. The woodland vegetation of Inchcailloch, Loch Lomond. Botanical Society of Edinburgh. Transactions, 42, 307-334.

HORSFALL, A.S., & KIRBY, K.J. 1985. The use of permanent quadrats to record changes in the structure and composition of Wytham Woods, Oxfordshire. Peterborough, Nature Conservancy Council (Research & survey in nature conservation No. 1).

HUNTER, F.A. 1977. Ecology of the pinewood beetles. In: Native pinewoods of Scotland, ed. by R.G.H. Bunce and J.N.R. Jeffers, 42-55. Cambridge, Institute of Terrestrial Ecology.

HUNTLEY, B., & BIRKS, H.J.B. 1977. The past and present vegetation of the Morrone Birkwoods, National Nature Reserve, Scotland. Journal of Ecology, 67, 417-467.

JAMES, N.D.G. 1981. A history of English forestry. Oxford, Blackwell.

JAMES, N.D.G. 1982. The forester's companion. 3rd ed. Oxford, Blackwell.

JAMES, P.W., HAWKSWORTH, D.L., & ROSE, F. 1977. Lichen communities in the British Isles: a preliminary conspectus. In: Lichen ecology, ed. by M.R.D. Seaward, 295-413. London, Academic Press.

JEFFERS, J.N.R. 1978a. Design of experiments. Statistical Check-list 1. Grange-over-Sands, Institute of Terrestrial Ecology.

JEFFERS, J.N.R. 1978b. Sampling. Statistical Check-list 2. Grange-over-Sands, Institute of Terrestrial Ecology.

JERMY, A.C., ARNOLD, H.R., FARRELL, L., & PERRING, F.H. 1978. Atlas of ferns of the British Isles. London, Botanical Society of the British Isles and British Pteridological Society.

JONES, E.W. 1945. The structure and reproduction of the virgin forests of the north temperate zone. New Phytologist, 44, 130-148.

KENNEDY, K.A., & ADDISON, P.A. 1987. Some considerations for the use of visual estimates of plant cover in biomonitoring. Journal of Ecology, 75, 151-158.

KERSHAW, K.A. 1973. Quantitative and dynamic plant ecology. 2nd ed. London, Arnold.

KING, C.M. 1975. The home range of the weasel, Mustela nivalis, in an English woodland. Journal of Animal Ecology, 44, 639-668.

KIRBY, K.J. 1980. Woodland evaluation and assessment for nature conservation purposes. Peterborough, Nature Conservancy Council (CST Note 25).

KIRBY, K.J. 1982. The broadleaved woodlands of the Duddon valley (Cumbria). Quarterly Journal of Forestry, 76, 83-91.

KIRBY, K.J. 1984a. Scottish birchwoods and their conservation. Botanical Society of Edinburgh. Transactions, 44, 205-218.

KIRBY, K.J. 1984b. A comparison of two methods for classifying British broadleaved woodland. Field Studies, 6, 103-116.

KIRBY, K.J. 1984c. Forestry operations and broadleaf woodland conservation. Peterborough, Nature Conservancy Council (Focus on nature conservation No. 8).

KIRBY, K.J. 1986. Forest and woodland evaluation. In: Wildlife conservation evaluation, ed. by M.B. Usher, 201-221. London, Chapman and Hall.

KIRBY, K.J., BINES, T., BURN, A., MACKINTOSH, J., PITKIN, P., & SMITH, I. 1986. Seasonal and observer differences in vascular plant records from British woodlands. Journal of Ecology, 74, 123-131.

KIRBY, K.J., PETERKEN, G.F., SPENCER, J.W., & WALKER, G.J. 1984. Inventories of ancient semi-natural woodland. Peterborough, Nature Conservancy Council (Focus on nature conservation No. 6).

KLOTZLI, F. 1970. [Oak, high quality broadleaved and swamp woods in the British Isles. Translation by H.J.B. Birks.] Schweizerische Zeitschrift fur das Forstwesen, 121, 329-366.

KOOP, H.G.J.M. 1986. Ecological monitoring of natural and semi-natural forests. In: Forest dynamics research in Western and Central Europe, ed. by J. Fanta, 257-262. Wageningen, Pudoc for IUFRO.

KRUUK, H., & PARISH, T. 1982. Factors affecting population density, group size and territory size of the European badger, Meles meles. Journal of Zoology, London, 196, 31-39.

LAKE DISTRICT SPECIAL PLANNING BOARD. 1978. The broadleaved woodlands of the Lake District. Kendal.

LANGDALE-BROWN, I., et al. 1980. Lowland agricultural habitats (Scotland): air-photo analysis of change. (Edinburgh University contract report). Peterborough, Nature Conservancy Council (CSD Research Report No. 332).

LEEMANS, R. 1986. Structure of the primaeval forest of Fiby. In: Forest dynamics research in Western and Central Europe, ed. by J. Fanta, 221-230. Wageningen, Pudoc for IUFRO.

LENTON, E.J., CHANIN, P.R.F., & JEFFERIES, D.J. 1980. Otter survey of England 1977-79. Peterborough, Nature Conservancy Council.

LEONARD, M. 1983. Base asymetry in stored-up oak coppice. Nature in Devon, 4, 29-33.

LINDLEY, D.K. 1976. Development of tree enumeration techniques. A data processing system. (ITE contract report). Peterborough, Nature Conservancy Council (CSD Research Report No. 56).

LINNARD, W. 1982. Welsh woods and forests: their history and utilisation. Cardiff, National Museum of Wales.

LINDSAY, J. 1983. A method of woodland mapping at large scales. Arboricultural Journal, 7, 53-62.

LLOYD, H.G. 1980. The red fox. London, Batsford.

LOCKE, G.M.L. 1970. Census of woodlands 1965-67. London, HMSO (for Forestry Commission).

LOCKE, G.M.L. 1987. Census of woodlands and trees 1979-82. London, HMSO (Forestry Commission Bulletin 63).

LOETSCH, F., ZOHRER, Z., & HALLER, K.E. 1973. Forest inventory. Munich, B.L.V. Verlags.

McVEAN, D.N., & RATCLIFFE, D.A. 1962. Plant communities of the Scottish Highlands. A study of Scottish mountain, moorland and forest vegetation. London, HMSO (Monographs of the Nature Conservancy No. 1).

MARCHANT, J.H. 1983. Common bird census instructions. Tring, British Trust for Ornithology.

MASSEY, M.E. 1974. The effect of woodland structure on the breeding bird communities in sample woods in south-central Wales. Nature in Wales, 14, 95-105.

MITCHELL, B., & COWAN, D. 1983. The faecal accumulation method for estimating and comparing populations of, and site occupation by red deer (Cervus elaphus L.). (ITE contract report). Peterborough, Nature Conservancy Council (CSD Research Report No. 489).

MOORE, P.D., & CHAPMAN, S.B. 1986. Methods in plant ecology. Oxford, Blackwell.

MORRIS, M.G., & PERRING, F.H., eds. 1974. The British oak. Faringdon, Classey.

MOSS, D. 1979. Even-aged plantations as a habitat for birds. In: The ecology of even-aged forest plantations, ed. by E.D. Ford, D.C. Malcolm and J. Atterson, 413-427. Cambridge, Institute of Terrestrial Ecology.

MUELLER-DOMBOIS, D., & ELLENBERG, H. 1974. Aims and methods of vegetation analysis. New York, Wiley.

MYERS, K., MARGULES, C.R., & MUSTO, I. 1983. Survey methods for nature conservation. Canberra, CSIRO.

NATURE CONSERVANCY COUNCIL. 1978. Photographic monitoring. Report of a working party of England staff. Banbury.

NEAL, E. 1986. The natural history of badgers. Beckenham, Croom Helm.

NEFF, D.J. 1968. The pellet group count technique for big game trend, census and distribution: a review. Journal of Wildlife Management, 32, 597-614.

O'CONNOR, R.J., & FULLER, R.J. 1984. A re-evaluation of the aims and methods of the Common Birds Census. (BTO contract report). Peterborough, Nature Conservancy Council (CSD Research Report No. 619).

OVINGTON, J.D. 1955. Studies of the development of woodland conditions under different trees. III. The ground flora. Journal of Ecology, 43, 1-21.

PARR, T.W. 1981. Scottish deciduous woodlands: a cause for concern. In: Forest and woodland ecology, ed. by F.T. Last and A.S. Grainger, 12-15. Cambridge, Institute of Terrestrial Ecology.

PEACHEY, C. 1980. The conservation of butterflies in Bernwood forest. Newbury, Nature Conservancy Council (unpublished).

PETERKEN, G.F. 1969. An event record for nature reserves. Devon Trust for Nature Conservation. Journal, 21, 920-928.

PETERKEN, G.F. 1974. A method for assessing woodland flora for conservation using indicator species. Biological Conservation, 6, 239-245.

PETERKEN, G.F. 1977a. Woodland survey for nature conservation. Peterborough, Nature Conservancy Council (CST Note 2).

PETERKEN, G.F. 1977b. Habitat conservation priorities in British and European woodlands. Biological Conservation, 11, 223-236.

PETERKEN, G.F. 1980. Classification of stand types in semi-natural woodland. Peterborough, Nature Conservancy Council (CST Note 23).

PETERKEN, G.F. 1981. Woodland conservation and management. London, Chapman and Hall.

PETERKEN, G.F. 1983. Woodland conservation in Britain. In: Conservation in perspective, ed. by A. Warren and F.B. Goldsmith, 83-100. London, Wiley.

PETERKEN, G.F., & ALLISON, H. In press. Habitat change: a review of changes in woodlands, hedges and non-woodland trees. Peterborough, Nature Conservancy Council.

PETERKEN, G.F., & GAME, M. 1984. Historical factors affecting the number and distribution of vascular plant species in the woodlands of central Lincolnshire. Journal of Ecology, 72, 155-182.

PETERKEN, G.F., & JONES, E.W. 1987. Forty years of change in Lady Park Wood: the old-growth stands. Journal of Ecology, 75, 477-512.

PETERKEN, G.F., & STACE, H. 1987. Stand development in the Black Wood of Rannock. Scottish Forestry, 41, 29-44.

PETERKEN, G.F., & WELCH, R.C. 1975. Bedford Purlieus: its history, ecology and management. Abbots Ripton, Institute of Terrestrial Ecology. (Monks Woods Experimental Station Symposium No. 7).

PIGOTT, C.D. 1969. The status of Tilia cordata and T. platyphyllos on the Derbyshire limestone. Journal of Ecology, 57, 491-504.

PIGOTT, C.D. 1983. Regeneration of oak-birch woodland following exclusion of sheep. Journal of Ecology, 71, 629-646.

POLLARD, E. 1977. A method for assessing changes in the abundance of butterflies. Biological Conservation, 12, 115-134.

POLLARD, E., HALL, M.L., & BIBBY, T.J. 1986. Monitoring the abundance of butterflies. Peterborough, Nature Conservancy Council (Research & survey in nature conservation No. 2).

PROCTOR, M.C.F., SPOONER, G.M., & SPOONER, M.F. 1980. Changes in Wistmans Woods, Dartmoor; photographic and other evidence. Devon Association for the Advancement of Science. Transactions, 112, 43-79.

PRYOR, S.N., & SAVILL, P.S. 1986. Silvicultural systems for broadleaved woodlands in Britain. Oxford, Oxford Forestry Institute (OFI Occasional Papers 32).

PUTMAN, R. 1986. Grazing in temperate ecosystems: large herbivores and the ecology of the New Forest. London, Croom Helm.

RACKHAM, O. 1975. Hayley Wood. Its history and ecology. Cambridge, Cambridgeshire and Isle of Ely Naturalists' Trust.

RACKHAM, O. 1976. Trees and woodland in the British landscape. London, Dent.

RACKHAM, O. 1980. Ancient woodland. London, Arnold.

RACKHAM, O. 1983. A review of "A field key for classifying British woodland vegetation". Journal of Ecology, 71, 648-649.

RACKHAM, O. 1986a. The history of the countryside. London, Dent.

RACKHAM, O. 1986b. The woods of south-east Essex. Rochford, Rochford District Council.

RATCLIFFE, D.A., ed. 1977. A nature conservation review. 2 vols. London, Cambridge University Press.

RALPH, C.J., & SCOTT, J.M. 1981. Estimating numbers of terrestrial birds. Studies in Avian Biology, 6. Lawrence, Kansas, Allen Press.

ROBERTSON, J.S. 1984. A key to the common plant communities of Scotland. Aberdeen, Macaulay Institute for Soil Research. (Soil Survey of Scotland Monograph).

ROSE, F. 1974. The epiphytes of oak. In: The British oak, ed. by M.G. Morris and F.H. Perring, 250-273. Faringdon, Classey.

ROSE, F. 1976. Lichenological indicators of age and environmental continuity in woodlands. In: Lichenology: progress and problems, ed. by D.H. Braun, D.L. Hawksworth and R.H.Bailey, 279-307. London, Academic Press.

RUSSELL, E.W. 1973. Soil conditions and plant growth. 10th ed. London, Longman.

SALISBURY, E.J. 1916. The oak-hornbeam woods of Hertfordshire. Journal of Ecology, 4, 83-120.

SEBER, G.A.F. 1982. The estimation of animal abundance and related parameters. London, Charles Griffin.

SHIMWELL, D.W. 1971. Description and classification of vegetation. London, Sidgwick and Jackson.

SMART, F.M., & GRAINGER, J.E.A. 1974. Sampling for vegetation survey: some aspects of the behaviour of unrestricted, restricted and stratified techniques. Journal of Biogeography, 1, 193-206.

SMART, N., & ANDREWS, J. 1985. Birds and broadleaves. Sandy, Royal Society for the Protection of Birds.

SMITH, I.R., WELLS, D.A., & WELSH, P. 1985. Botanical survey and monitoring methods for grasslands. Peterborough, Nature Conservancy Council (Focus on conservation No. 10).

SMITH, M.A. 1981. Broadleaved woodlands in East Gwynedd. Survey evaluation and site selection. Bangor, Nature Conservancy Council (unpublished).

SMITH, R. 1900. Botanical survey of Scotland. II. North Perthshire District. Scottish Geographical Magazine, 16, 441-467.

SMITH, W.G. 1904. Botanical survey of Scotland. Forfar and Fife Districts. Scottish Geographical Magazine, 20, 4-23, 57-83, 117-126.

SNEDECOR, G.W., & COCHRAN, W.G. 1967. Statistical methods. Ames, Iowa, Iowa State University Press.

SOUTHWOOD, T.R.E. 1978. Ecological methods. London, Chapman and Hall.

STAMP, L.D. 1948, 1950, 1962. The land of Britain, its use and misuse. London, Longman.

STEEL, D. 1984. Shotover. The natural history of a Royal forest. Oxford, Pisces.

STEELE, R.C., & PETERKEN, G.F. 1982. Management objectives for broadleaved woodland - conservation. In: Broadleaves in Britain: future management and research, ed. by D.C. Malcolm, J. Evans and P.N. Edwards, 91-103. Edinburgh, Institute of Chartered Foresters.

STEELE, R.C., & WELCH, R.C. 1973. Monks Wood. A nature reserve record. Huntingdon, Nature Conservancy.

STEVEN, H.M., & CARLISLE, A. 1959. The native pinewoods of Scotland. Edinburgh, Oliver and Boyd.

STUBBS, A.E. 1972. Wildlife conservation and dead wood. Devon Trust for Nature Conservation. Quarterly Journal, 4, 169-182.

STUBBS, A.E. 1979. Guidelines to invertebrate conservation. Peterborough, Nature Conservancy Council (CST Note 17).

SYKES, J.M. 1976. A vegetation survey of Wood of Cree SSSI, Kirkcudbrightshire. (ITE contract report). Peterborough, Nature Conservancy Council (CSD Research Report No. 75).

SYKES, J.M. 1981. Monitoring in woodlands. In: Forest and woodland ecology, ed. by F.T. Last and A.S. Grainger, 32-40. Cambridge, Institute of Terrestrial Ecology.

SYKES, J.M., & HORRILL, A.D. 1979. Survey methods within woodlands. (ITE contract report). Peterborough, Nature Conservancy Council (unpublished).

SYKES, J.M., & HORRILL, A.D. 1985. Natural regeneration in a Caledonian Pinewood: progress after eight years of enclosure at Coille Coire Chuilc. Arboricultural Journal, 9, 13-24.

SYKES, J.M., HORRILL, A.D., & MOUNTFORD, M.D. 1983. Use of visual cover assessments as quantitative estimators in some British woodland taxa. Journal of Ecology, 71, 427-450.

SYKES, J.M., MARRS, R.H., & MITCHELL, B. 1985. The impact of red deer (Cervus elaphus L.) on the vegetation of native Scottish pinewoods: selection of sites for further studies using the faecal accumulation method, and recommendations for sampling vegetation. (ITE contract report). Peterborough, Nature Conservancy Council (CSD Research Report No. 571).

TAMM, C.O. 1956. Further observations on the survival of some perennial herbs. Oikos, 7, 273-292.

TANSLEY, A.G. 1939. The British Islands and their vegetation. Cambridge, Cambridge University Press.

TEE, L.A., ROWE, J.J., & PEPPER, H.W. 1985. Mammal and bird damage questionnaire 1983. Edinburgh, Forestry Commission (Research & Development Paper 137).

THOMAS, J.A. 1983. A quick method for estimating butterfly numbers during surveys. Biological Conservation, 27, 195-212.

TITTENSOR, R.M. 1970. History of the Loch Lomond oakwoods. Scottish Forestry, 24, 100-118.

TOMIALOJC, L. 1980. The combined version of the mapping method. In: Bird census work and nature conservation. Proceedings of the VI International Conference on Bird Census and Atlas work, ed. by H.Oelke, 92-106.

TROUP, R.S. 1952. Silvicultural systems. 2nd ed., ed. by E.W. Jones. Oxford, Oxford University Press.

TUBBS, C.R. 1964. The New Forest: an ecological history. Newton Abbott, David and Charles.

TUBBS, C.R. 1986. The New Forest: a natural history. London, Collins (New Naturalist).

USHER, M.B., ed. 1986. Wildlife conservation evaluation. London, Chapman and Hall.

VELANDER, K.A. 1983. Pine marten survey of Scotland, England and Wales, 1980-82. London, Vincent Wildlife Trust.

WALKER, G.J., & KIRBY, K.J. 1987. An historical approach to woodland conservation in Scotland. Scottish Forestry, 41, 87-98.

WALTON, R. 1985. A Phase I habitat mapping handbook. Peterborough, Nature Conservancy Council (unpublished).

WATKINS, C. 1984. The use of Forestry Commission censuses for the study of woodland change. Journal of Historical Geography, 10, 396-406.

WATKINS, C. 1985. Sources for the assessment of British woodland change in the twentieth century. Applied Geography, 5, 151-166.

WATSON, W. 1953. Census catalogue of British lichens. London, Cambridge University Press for British Mycological Society.

WATT, A.S. 1925. On the ecology of British beechwoods with special reference to their regeneration. Part II, Sections II and III. The development and structure of beech communities on the Sussex Downs (continued). Journal of Ecology, 13, 27-73.

WHITE, R.E. 1979. Introduction to the principles and practice of soil science. Oxford, Blackwell.

WHITEHEAD, D. 1982. Ecological aspects of natural and plantation forests. Forestry Abstracts, 43, 615-624.

WIGGINTON, M.J., & GRAHAM, G.G. 1981. Guide to the identification of some of the more difficult vascular plant species. Banbury, Nature Conservancy Council (England Field Unit Occasional Paper No. 1).

WILLIAMSON, K. 1964. Bird census work in woodlands. Bird Study, 11, 1-22.

WILLIAMSON, K. 1970. Birds and modern forestry. Quarterly Journal of Forestry, 64, 346-355.

WILLIAMSON, K. 1976. Bird life in the Wood of Cree, Galloway. Quarterly Journal of Forestry, 70, 206-215.

WOODROFFE-PEACOCK, E.A. 1918. A fox-covert study. Journal of Ecology, 6, 110-125.